A Tale of Tw

Michael Goulder

A Tale of
Two Missions

SCM PRESS LTD

0 334 02363 7

First published 1994
by SCM Press Ltd
26–30 Tottenham Road, London N1 4BZ

Phototypeset by Intype, London
and printed in Great Britain by
Biddles Ltd, Guildford and King's Lynn

for Clare,
to whose encouragement I owe so much,
and to whose restraint I might have been
wise to owe more.

Contents

Introduction

'They used to call the church a virgin', wrote Hegesippus in the
second century, 'for she had not yet been corrupted by vain teachings';
and the virgin-church theory has been held by most Christians ever
since, simple believers and scholars alike. Of course the scholars
hold a sophisticated form of the hypothesis: there were varied
anonymous groupings within the church – the Jesus movement, the
Q community, the proto-gnostics and so on – but essentially the
New Testament was the developing statement of the experience of
the one virginal church. The first disciples had the unique experience
of the human Jesus, then of the resurrection, then of the Holy Spirit.
Before Paul these experiences were already expressed in prayers and
hymns. Paul thought these pre-Pauline ideas through, and wrote his
own conclusions in the Epistles. The evangelists had access to the
memories of the first disciples, and they re-told the traditions
about Jesus in the Gospels, either in line with, or modifying, the
Pauline theology. The false teachers who cloud the later books
of the New Testament are a mixture of out-of-date 'Judaizers',
gnostics, syncretists and other menaces who tried to seduce the
virginal church. The whole structure of Christian belief grew,
as Cardinal Newman was so memorably to put it, as an oak out of
an acorn.

This book is an attempt to show that the acorn-oak, virgin-in-
peril theory is an error. From as far back as we can trace it (to the
40s) there never was a single, united church. There were (in fact
from the 30s) two missions: one run from Jerusalem, with Peter and
the sons of Zebedee in charge, and later James, Jesus' brother, and
other members of his family; the other run by Paul, from various
centres. The two missions were agreed about the supreme signifi-

cance of Jesus, but they disagreed about almost everything else – the validity of the Bible, whether the kingdom of God had arrived or not, sex, money, work, tongues, visions, healings, Jesus' divinity, and the resurrection of the dead, for example. The New Testament gives the impression of a united, developing body of belief because it is a *selection* of writings; naturally it was selected by the winning mission, that is the Paulines, and that is why it consists of the Epistles of Paul (and his followers), and four Gospels, two of them ultra-Pauline and two building bridges to Jerusalem.

This book attempts to tell the story of the two missions from as early as our evidence takes us, in practice AD 48, and runs on to about 130, with some raids on later material. There are no anonymous hypothetical groups in it. Of course there were many sub-divisions of opinion within the church, but I have kept to the central cleft, where we know the names of the leaders, and have direct evidence. All evidence has to be interpreted, and my interpretations, like those of other scholars, are open to dispute; but I have kept to the documents we have, and have eschewed hypothetical sources (pre-Pauline hymns, Q, M, L, proto-Thomas, etc.), in whose existence I do not believe. I have relied more than other scholars on three arguments, which have resulted in a conclusion substantially different from theirs: *coherence*, in that I have drawn evidence from all the major New Testament and some other sources into a single overall picture; a *loyalty test*, by which the sympathies of each author may be revealed towards the two leaderships; and the *emphatic negative*, by which it is inferred that some other Christian is asserting what is repeatedly denied.

For every reader of the New Testament the first problem is to see the connections between the Epistles and the Gospels. The usual way of doing this is to read both against the background of Acts; but this is, as they know, the path to bewilderment. How, to give an example, are we to reconcile Jesus' clear teaching to Peter and others that all food is clean (Mark 7.15–19) with Peter's need of a vision proclaiming 'What God has cleansed do not call unclean' (Acts 10), and then, some years later, Peter's refusal to eat meat at Antioch (Gal.2.12)? Acts is in fact a doubtful asset, for it was Luke who invented the united virginal church theory, and Acts is his steady and skilful attempt to paper over all the cracks. We could not tell the story of the two missions without Acts, but it is Paul who is our primary source: Paul was there at the time. It is the Epistles which enable us to see what is going on in the churches in the 50s, and we have then to use this picture to interpret the different emphases which we find in the Gospels, and which are so revealing.

The book tries to tell the story of the early church, and the New Testament which it produced. It does not attempt the much more difficult task of isolating what Jesus taught. That takes us into deep waters which I have attempted to sail elsewhere; but the reader may wish to know what I have presupposed here. There certainly were traditions of Jesus' sayings which have come through into our four Gospels; but it has been common ground for a century that John put these teachings into his own words, and felt free to reinterpret them in line with his own theology. It has become widely agreed more recently that the other three evangelists used some similar licence or freedom. What is at issue is how much, and here I am rather on the radical end of the spectrum: I think that all four evangelists felt free to put the tradition in their own (Greek) words, and thought that it was their duty to do so, in the same way that contemporary Jews retold the biblical stories. So it is perilous to infer that Jesus said something from the fact that one or more of the Gospels said he did; but it is usually safe to think that each evangelist wrote what he himself believed to be true. The Gospels almost always give us the theology of their authors, and sometimes true tradition about Jesus.

The Two Missions theory has been twenty years in development, and I present it here in a form intended for anyone – sixth-form students, first year undergraduates, theological students, the general reader: what Bernard Shaw called the intelligent woman, but one has to be so careful these days. I have limited the evidence expounded, I have made the chapters short, I have left out virtually all footnotes, and I have tried to write with a little wit and some feeling. But I hope that this informality will not lead my professional colleagues to overlook the work; it says something with which most of them have not come to terms. If they require footnotes, the references are in Appendix II. If they would prefer an 800 page statement, I am preparing one.

The quotations of the Bible in this book are my own translations based on the Revised Standard Version.

November, 1993   Michael Goulder

I

The Basic Tension

The earliest incidents in church history of which we have a first-hand account reveal an uncomfortable tension. Paul had been a leading member of the church at Antioch, in Syria, for some years, and the mission there had been successful in converting some Gentiles (non-Jews). The question had then arisen as to how much of the Jewish Law in the Bible these Gentile converts needed to keep; and Paul had adopted a liberal policy – roughly speaking they had (of course) to keep the *moral* commandments, but he turned a blind eye over the *ceremonial* commandments, other than central matters like idolatry. This decision then led to a series of difficult incidents, which he records in the letter that he wrote some years later to the Galatian churches, in central Turkey. The first of these happened a dozen years or so after his conversion:

> Then after fourteen years I went up again to Jerusalem with Barnabas, taking Titus also with us. I went up by revelation . . . because of false brethren secretly brought in, who slipped in to spy out our freedom which we have in Christ Jesus, that they might bring us into bondage – to them we did not yield submission for a moment (Gal. 2.1–4).

The 'false brethren' were Christians from Jerusalem, 350 miles away. They had been sent to see what was going on at Antioch, and naturally had not mentioned this at first. However, when they realized that the Antioch church was not observing the Jewish Law (especially, as it turns out, over kosher meat), they raised an objection. Paul refused to change his church's ways ('to them we did not yield submission for a moment'), and regarded them as having deceived him ('false brethren secretly brought in, who slipped in to spy out our freedom which we have in Christ Jesus'). As they could *spy* it *out*, it must have been something they could see, like the meat.

The 'false brethren' then reported the lax ways of the Antioch church to the Jerusalem apostles, who wanted proper order observed. Paul saw trouble coming ('I went up by revelation'), and took Barnabas and Titus, a young Greek Christian, with him to talk the apostles round. He saw James (Jesus' brother), Peter and John, and he speaks of them in a rather sarcastic tone: 'those who are reputed to be something (what they are makes no difference to me; God shows no impartiality) . . . those who seemed to be pillars' (2.6,9). The ill temper with which he speaks of them is a clear indication that he saw them behind the further, extensive trouble which the letter to the Galatians was written to counter.

The Jerusalem meeting was in fact friendly, and the cracks were papered over; but the underlying tension soon reappeared:

> But when Cephas came to Antioch I opposed him to the face because he stood condemned. For before certain men came from James he ate with the Gentiles; but when they came he drew back and separated himself, fearing those of the circumcision. And with him the rest of the Jews acted hypocritically, so that even Barnabas was carried away with their hypocrisy. But when I saw that they were not straightforward about the truth of the gospel, I said to Cephas before them all, 'If you, though a Jew, live like a Gentile and not like a Jew, how can you compel the Gentiles to live like Jews?' (Gal. 2.11–14).

Cephas is another name for Peter: Jesus had given him the name 'Rock', which is *Cepha* in Aramaic and *Petros* in Greek. He had come to Antioch because James and he were not too sure of what was going on there, and felt they had better see for themselves. At first Peter enjoyed the friendly atmosphere and the devotion of the church, and he joined in eating the meat at the church supper, without asking any questions about where it had been bought or how it had been cooked ('he ate with the Gentiles'). But James in Jerusalem suspected that Peter's kindly heart meant that he would not put his foot down; so he sent a further deputation ('certain men from James'), and they found, just as James feared, that he was not insisting on kosher meat, purity laws, etc. ('living like a Gentile'). So they said to him quietly, 'Look here, which side are you on?'

The following Saturday night there was a scene. Peter said, 'Before we go any further, I have to ask, Is this meat kosher? Was it bought at the Jewish butcher's?' Well, the meat actually came from the Antioch market; so Peter said, 'Then I'm afraid that all God's people will have to go next door for the Eucharist ("separated themselves"); and leave this meat for those who have not yet put themselves under God's Law'. It was a moment of crisis: everyone there had to decide whether Peter or Paul was right. Paul naturally hoped that his church would stand solidly with him, but in fact all the Jewish members had been feeling guilty of breaking the Law, and they sided with Peter; even Paul's closest ally Barnabas felt that was right ('was carried away by their hypocrisy'). This naturally made Paul very angry, because in effect his Gentile converts were being excommunicated; so he explained to Peter where he had gone wrong ('I withstood him to the face because he stood condemned'). Before the James party arrived he had joined in and eaten the non-kosher meat ('lived like a Gentile'); now that they had frightened him, he was trying to force Jewish ways on the Gentile Christians ('compel them to live like Jews'). This was a double life, or hypocrisy; but the die had been cast by now, and the Peter party, the *Petrines*, had won the round.

In the long run the Paulines won, and Christians today do not have to eat kosher meat or be circumcised. In consequence non-Jewish readers of the story usually sympathize with Paul, and are apt to speak of the Jerusalem Christian attitude as pettifogging, legalistic, trivial, etc. But if we are to follow the story open-mindedly, we must be fair to James and Peter. If you accept the Bible as the word of God (as they all did, Paul included), then it is not for you to say that one of God's rules, say not murdering, is important, and another, circumcision, is pettifogging: if God has said it is to be done, that is the end of the matter. Furthermore, many of the rules may need some explanation. Leviticus 17.14 says that you may not eat blood in your meat: well, what exactly are you to do to make sure there is *no* blood? Sometimes one text says one thing and one another, as Henry VIII discovered when he wished to have his marriage with his dead brother's wife annulled. If God has told us what he wishes us to do, then surely we must have such points discussed by experts, and we must follow their conclusions. That is what the Jewish Sages had been doing for centuries, and Peter and James were honouring God's word by taking their interpretations seriously. Paul, on the other hand, knew that the Gentile church-members would be repelled by a demand that they should observe such rulings, and he thought it was obvious that they did not apply now Christ had come: so he speaks of 'our freedom which we have in Christ Jesus', and of 'bringing us into bondage', and he calls Peter and the others hypocrites because they had first joined in and then withdrawn.

Although the issue about Jewish rulings has faded away, the point about interpreting the Bible has not, and a modern example may help the non-Jewish reader to balance his sympathies. The film *Chariots of Fire* featured the partially true story of the Scottish runner, Eric Liddell, who was picked to run for the United Kingdom in the Paris Olympics of 1924, and declined to run because the heat was on a Sunday. He was a pious Presbyterian Christian, later a missionary, who would not break the sabbath. The Bible law is set out in Ex. 20.8, 'Remember the sabbath day, to keep it holy', and for Liddell that settled the question, let the Prince of Wales say what he would. Now the attentive reader may notice that *two* steps have been jumped in the argument. First, Exodus goes on to say that the sabbath (rest) day is to be kept on the *seventh* day of the week, that is *Saturday*; so Sunday activities are not covered at all. Secondly, while Exodus clearly forbids work on the sabbath, no mention is made of *running* as work. But Prince Edward was well advised not to try either of these arguments, which would have seemed sophistries to Liddell. When people have been brought up in a long and unchallenged religious environment, the community's interpretations of its traditions have all the authority of the Bible itself. So although secular modern man may think gold medals more important than fusty old superstitions, he can still empathize with Liddell, and admire his integrity; and he ought (and even more ought the religious man) to empathize with and admire James and Peter for their integrity.

The problem between them and Paul was one which would not go away in a hurry. Here is Ignatius, a Pauline, the Bishop of Antioch seventy years later; he is on his way to be martyred in Rome, and the scene is Philadelphia in modern Turkey, not far from the Galatian churches Paul had been writing to:

> If anyone propound Judaism to you, do not listen to him . . . For even though certain persons desired to deceive me after the flesh, the spirit is not deceived . . . I cried out, when I was among you; I spoke with a loud voice, with God's own voice, 'Give heed to the bishop and the presbytery and deacons' . . . I heard certain people saying, 'If I do not find it in the ancient texts, I do not believe it in the Gospel'; and when I said to them, 'It is written', they answered me, 'That is the question' (*Philadelphians*, 6ff.).

The Philadelphian church is split. It has 'Jewish Christians' in it, who *propound Judaism* and trust only the Old Testament, the *ancient texts*; and it has Gentile Christians, who do not keep the Jewish food laws, circumcision, etc., and who have some other, Christian book, which Ignatius calls 'the Gospel'. Perhaps this is St John's Gospel, which he has just quoted. Ignatius has come as a stranger to the church, and the Jewish party has kept quiet (*desired to deceive me*); but he had met this kind of tension before, and he soon guessed what was up. Now Paul used to run a mission for a short period and then move on, normally; and when he left, he used to appoint a committee of senior people ('the presbytery') and other officers ('deacons') to run the church. In time the most senior person, often the one in whose house the church met, became known as the 'overseer' (Greek *episcopos*) or bishop. So Ignatius shouts out that the church should follow these leaders, or in other words, the Pauline party; and like some modern preachers, he thinks that if he shouts it loud it is because he is inspired (*God's own voice*). All this then leads to the friendly exchange which follows.

These are two first-hand accounts of Christian church meetings, from either end of the period which this book covers. The row between Paul and Peter happened in about 48; the one between Ignatius and the Jewish Christians at Philadelphia took place about 117. None of our New Testament books was written before the dispute at Antioch, and most had been written before Ignatius' martyrdom. It is not an accident that they both reveal the same basic tension, for this tension was certain to appear wherever the Pauline mission went. For there were Jews in every major centre throughout the Roman Empire, and Paul's normal preaching method was to go to the synagogue first. Even if he did not convert some Jews, the Gentiles whom he won over had been used to Jewish ways and respected the Old Testament as the word of God. But Paul knew that the Gentile mission would never go far if it got tied up with kosher meat and tithing rules; and he was totally persuaded that Christ had died to save all mankind. So everywhere it was inevitable that there would be divisions on this issue. Of course there might be many other divisions, but this division was bound to come. There were two missions: the Jerusalem mission headed by Jesus' central disciples, Peter, James and John, and by Jesus' family, his brothers James, Jude and the others; and the Pauline mission, headed by Paul, with centres first at Antioch, later at Ephesus in western Turkey, and finally in Europe. This book is an account of the first century of church life in the light of this basic split.

Most people today live in tolerant communities. It is not inevitable that there should be bad blood in England between black and white, English and Gaelic, Jew and Gentile; and we do not easily allow the force of the word 'inevitable'. But a visit to Ulster should open the eyes. The story of the English official who landed at Belfast is symbolic, if apocryphal. The reporter asked, 'Are you a Catholic or a Protestant?', and after a moment the official replied, 'I'm an atheist'; to which the reporter answered, 'Yes, but are you a Catholic atheist or a Protestant atheist?' In some communities there is an issue which you cannot escape; and when national and religious identity are involved, as they were with the Petrine and Pauline missions, you have issues for which men will die, and kill. It is probable that both Paul and Ignatius died in partial consequence of the hatred of Jewish Christians (that is, those loyal to Peter and James); and we shall see that the Paulines, especially St John, hated the Jewish Christians with an equal ferocity.

There are other suggestions than the one which you will read here to explain the tensions underlying the New Testament; but this is the only one for which there is direct support in the New Testament text. The two missions are there in Galatians, with their leaders: 'when they saw that I had been entrusted with the gospel to the uncircumcision [the non-Jews] as Peter had been with the gospel to the circumcision; for he who authorized *Peter for the mission to the circumcision authorized me too for the mission to the Gentiles*' (2.7f.). The issue about the Law is the subject of Paul's letters to the Galatians and the Romans, and crops up in virtually every other book in one form or another. But the Law was only the first of many differences between the two missions; and to understand what those differences were, and why they arose, is to understand the New Testament.

2

The Loyalty Test I: Jesus' Family and the Sons of Zebedee

The early church was not short of leadership. There were the *Twelve*, who had been with Jesus. When Paul goes up to Jerusalem (Gal. 1.18; 2.1) he finds only Peter (and John) there; so it is likely that *Peter, James and John*, the sons of Zebedee, ran the Jerusalem church at first, while the *Nine* supervised things in Galilee. However, quite soon Jesus' family arrived in Jerusalem, and *James the brother of the Lord* became progressively the leader in the church there (Gal. 1.19; 2.9, where he is mentioned first; Acts 12.17; 15.13, where he seems to be chairman; 21.18, where Peter seems to be missing); there were other brothers too (I Cor. 9.5), and after James was martyred in 62, Jesus' cousin Symeon became bishop (Hegesippus, in Eusebius, *Ecclesiastical History* 3.11–12). All these people spoke Aramaic. But there soon arose a semi-independent, Greek-speaking church, whose leaders were *Stephen and Philip*, and in time *Paul and Barnabas*. So it is not surprising if there was a little tension.

Paul was a decent man who wanted to get on with the Jerusalem leadership, the *pillars*, as they called themselves (Gal. 2.9). He says, humbly, 'I laid before them . . . the gospel which I preach among the Gentiles, lest somehow I should be running or had run in vain' (2.2) – he didn't want his energy wasted. But the tension was one of principle, as we have already seen: the revealed Law of God on the one side, and the souls of the Gentile millions on the other. It was a not uneven struggle. The pillars had the authority of having been chosen by Jesus, and the authority of the Bible, which both sides agreed to be infallible; and in 48 they were running a scatter of churches with perhaps five thousand members, while Paul was pastor of a single church at Antioch with perhaps fifty. But Paul was better educated than they were, and he was a brilliant thinker; and he was possessed by an overmastering conviction that he was called by God. Convictions are always more powerful than institutions, and it was Paul who triumphed.

When things were going his way, Paul could speak kindly of the pillars. In I Cor. there is a group 'of Cephas' competing with his converts, and he can handle the argument tactfully (I Cor. 1.12–16). He is fretted by the suggestion that Peter is the foundation *rock* of the church in ch. 3, and speaks roughly about his followers. But when things are going against him, he can turn sarcastic and nasty. He lost the Antioch church to Peter and the others (ch. 1), and it looked as if they were going to force the hands of his Galatian converts too. Hence they became 'those who were reputed to be something (what they were makes no difference to me – God shows no partiality)' (Gal. 2.6). In II Corinthians he calls them 'super-apostles' (11.5; 12.11), and he calls their emissaries 'false apostles, deceitful workers, disguising themselves as apostles of Christ' (11.13). In Philippians such people are called dogs (3.2). What upset him most was the constant charge that he was not an *apostle*. The word means missionary, one sent (Greek *apostello*), and the Twelve reckoned that applied to them only: Matthew says, 'The names of the *twelve apostles* are these . . .' (10.2). But Paul felt certain that he had been sent by Jesus on the Damascus road; he often starts his letters, 'Paul an apostle', and is liable to say indignantly, 'Am I not an apostle? Have I not seen Jesus our Lord?' (I Cor. 9.1). But stressing Paul's inferiority was the Petrines' best weapon.

To understand the New Testament it is essential to know which side the various authors are on, Paul's or the Jerusalem leaders'; and the way to find out is a *loyalty test*. We are familiar with this technique in modern life with political issues. You are invited to a dinner party and somebody tells a story about Mr Kinnock being arrested by black soldiers in Africa, and everyone laughs: well, that tells you (if you did not know already) that the company votes Conservative. You hear someone say, 'I hear the SDP is holding its annual Conference in a telephone box in Plymouth': the author of this remark was Mr Tony Benn, but anyone repeating it is Labour, because only Labour voters hate the SDP as traitors to the cause. It is important to notice that it is quite immaterial whether the story is true. Mr Kinnock *was* detained in Africa: Dr Owen did *not* plan his Conference in a phone box. The point is that people only tell discreditable stories when they wish the person concerned to lose credit. Sometimes they may *have* to tell a discreditable story because everyone knows it, and then they try to make the story *less* discreditable. When you have several accounts of the same incident, as we do in the Gospels, you can soon tell where the author's sympathies lie. So we apply the test by forgetting for the moment the interesting (and often unanswerable) question, 'What really happened?', and concentrating on the prior question, 'What is the story-teller's attitude?'

The Gospels do not tell stories about Paul, for obvious reasons; but they do tell stories about the Jerusalem leaders, and we may suitably start with Jesus' brothers, because it was his family that was running the Jerusalem church when the Gospels were written. Mark has three mentions of them:

> And when his family heard (of Jesus' success), they went out to seize him; for they said, He is out of his mind (3.21).

A few verses later they arrive:

> And his mother and his brothers came; and standing outside they sent to him and called him. And a crowd was sitting round him; and they said to him, Your mother and your brothers are outside asking for you. And he replied, Who are my mother and my brothers? And looking about at those sitting round him he said, Here are my mother and my brothers. Whoever does the will of God is my brother and sister and mother (3.31–35).

After two chapters Jesus comes to preach at his home town Nazareth, and it is a failure. Jesus comments philosophically:

> A prophet is not without honour, except in his own country, and among his own relatives, and in his own house (6.4).

Now at first sight all these passages sound *hostile* to Jesus' family. In 3.21 they react negatively to his success, they think he is mad, and they go out to stop him forcibly. When they arrive, we have what looks like a picture of the early church: a crowd gathered in a house, all sitting round Jesus who is teaching them. The family do not belong with this embryonic church: they are twice said to be standing *outside*. Jesus says that his (true) family are those who do the will of God, that is his followers. At Nazareth the people who do not honour Jesus include his *relatives* and his *'house'*; and his house means his family, his mother and brothers.

This is an unexpected and unwelcome conclusion; and it is not surprising that many devout Christians have not liked it. Surely, they may feel, our Lady will have remembered what the archangel told her . . . So many translations have tried to soften the harsh words Mark uses. 'His family' becomes 'his friends'; 'they said' becomes 'people were saying'; 'He is out of his mind' becomes 'He is beside himself' – and so on; and some commentaries speak of 'affectionate restraint'. But the impression made by the whole is consistent, and should not be resisted for reasons of piety. Mark must have a reason for telling these stories like this; and it could perhaps be that he is a Pauline who is trying to counter constant assertions by Jerusalem Christians that the leaders of the church were Jesus' family, and Paulines should do what they said. He might be countering this by saying, 'Well, Jesus' family were not much use to him in his lifetime'. And perhaps he had never heard of the virginal conception.

All this is hypothesis; but it is rather confirmed by Matthew's and Luke's retelling of the same stories. Both of these later evangelists usually retain everything that comes in Mark (especially Matthew does), but both of them leave out the verse about the family thinking Jesus was mad. This is doubly suggestive. It implies that they are both *more friendly* to Jesus' family; and it also implies that Mark could have left the detail out if he had wanted to. They both include the following scene, but the sting is now drawn. Matthew drops the suggestion that they were trying to 'call' Jesus away from his mission, and says they were 'asking to speak to him' (12.46). Luke says, even more nicely, 'they could not reach him for the crowd' (8.19). Without the madness verse, the story reads innocuously in both Gospels: Jesus' family were all in the mission, and wanted to be close to him. Matthew and Luke both take the sting out of the Nazareth story too. Matthew has 'A prophet is not without honour except in his own country and in his own house' (13.57): where have *the relatives* gone? Luke has gone even further: 'no prophet is acceptable in his own country' (4.24). He has dropped both the relatives and Jesus' house(hold) too.

When we look at a series of little details like this, we are forming working theories about the writers' concerns, or *tendencies*. Both Matthew and Luke seem to have a tendency to exonerate Jesus' family; and we could explain this by the view that they were both much more sympathetic to the Jerusalem church than Mark was. In the case of Luke, we really know that this was so, because we have a second book Luke wrote, the Acts of the Apostles. In that book Peter (and the other Eleven) are the heroes in chs 1–12, and Paul is the hero in chs 13–28; and in ch. 15, when the issue of Gentiles keeping the Law is discussed, everyone agrees with Paul, and the Gentiles are not made to observe it. So we know that Luke is a liberal Pauline: he is on Paul's side when the chips are down (and was probably Paul's doctor and companion), but he wants the church united and the two missions reconciled, and he will not tell stories in which Jesus' family come out badly. Matthew is not quite so easy to label, but I will suggest reasons for thinking that he was a liberal Petrine.

It is important to remember that these suggestions are only *working hypotheses*; they have to be checked with further evidence, and we may look next at the other James, the son of Zebedee, and John his brother. This time things are more complicated, because the evidence in Mark points in both directions. In some respects Peter, James and John are the heroes of the story. They are the first three to be called, with Andrew, and they courageously leave their living at Jesus' call; they alone are taken in by Jesus to be present at the raising of Jairus' daughter; they alone are taken up the mountain and see Jesus transfigured; they, with Andrew, are given the secrets of the things to come; they alone are asked by Jesus to pray in Gethsemane. But against this there are two stories which show James and John in a bad light. At Mark 10.35 they are portrayed as ambitious and unspiritual by asking Jesus to sit on either side of him in heaven; and at 9.38 John (without James), appears as narrow-minded because he tries to stop a man casting out demons in Jesus' name.

In some ways it is the last two incidents which make the greater impact, partly because they are longer, and partly because these are the only times when the brothers appear without Peter. In Mark 10 they ask for the highest places, causing the ten to be indignant; and

Jesus takes six verses to rebuke them – are they prepared to share Jesus' martyrdom?; exercising authority is a thing for worldly rulers, but it will not be so in the church; the Son of Man (Jesus) came not to be served but to serve.

The passage in ch. 9 is related, and is even longer (9.33–50). The disciples have been discussing which of them was the greatest – the same point – and Jesus humbles them by setting a child in their midst. John then says he has stopped the exorcist from using Jesus' name 'because he was not following us', and he is told:

> Do not forbid him; for no one who does a mighty work in my name will be able to speak evil of me. For he who is not against us is for us. For truly I say to you, whoever gives you a cup of water to drink because you bear the name of Christ will by no means lose his reward. Whoever causes one of these little ones who believe in me to stumble, it would be better for him if a great millstone were hung round his neck and he were thrown into the sea. And if your hand causes you to stumble, cut it off; it is better for you to enter life maimed than with two hands to go to hell . . .

At first sight the thread is hard to follow; but the line of thought is easy to see from the position I have outlined. The Jerusalem leaders were very keen on *authority*; they felt they were the true leaders of the church, the *greatest*. Paulines like Mark did not accept their authority, and represented it as unspiritual ambition. In particular they tried to stop the great Pauline mission to the Gentiles, because it was not under their control – at least John did; James had been executed in 43, and Peter had been a bit more friendly. So Mark remembered the little incident of the exorcist whom John had tried to stop. The moral drawn is that others (like Paul) who *do not follow us*, who are not under Jerusalem's control, are also on Jesus' side. In fact anyone who helps a missionary on his way will be counted in; and woe betide any church leader (like those in Jerusalem) who drive out new converts (*little ones who believe in me*) by insisting on Jewish rules (*causing them to stumble*). Such leaders would be better drowned; anything they hold precious would be better cut off rather than that they should go to hell.

What about the positive stories then? Well, we are often in the position of feeling two ways about people. American Democrats wanted to vote Mr Bush out of office; but they were proud of what he had done in Kuwait. Earlier some of them would have liked Senator Edward Kennedy for President; but it might be necessary to give some account of what happened at Chappaquiddick. So with Mark. A lot of Christians knew that Peter, James and John had been an inner circle of Jesus' followers; and Paulines too were grateful for their having set the Jerusalem church up in the 30s – indeed, for keeping the movement going after the crucifixion. So Mark might be glad to include traditional stories about the Three which were to their credit. But when it came to the important, contemporary issue, 'Were the Jerusalem leadership *the greatest?* Did Jesus want them to *exercise authority?* Should they *forbid* others who were taking Jesus' name but not *following them?* What about *The little ones who believed in him* whom they with their rulings *made to stumble?*, Mark's principles asserted themselves. Jerusalem Christians who were forever boasting that their authority derived from the Three had to be put severely in their place. James and John had been a couple of classic authoritarians, and Jesus had said as much, and warned them that they were on the way to hell for it.

As with the stories about Jesus' family, we find Matthew and Luke much less hostile. Matthew leaves out the incident of John and the exorcist altogether. Instead of James and John asking for the best seats in the kingdom, he has *their mother* come and ask instead: we all know how embarrassing mothers can be! Luke leaves out the latter story; he transfers some of the sayings about authority to the Last Supper, but he does not mention James and John at all. The exorcist story is cut down in Luke to just two verses; all the moral about accepting other initiatives, and all the threats, are dropped. So the poison is drawn, and in both Matthew and Luke the sons of Zebedee appear as heroes; rather impetuous heroes in Luke, for they suggest calling down fire from heaven on some unwelcoming villagers – but then did not Jesus call them the Sons of Thunder?

So we begin to get a picture, still a *provisional* picture, of the alignment of the evangelists in the early church's battles. Mark looks like a Pauline, hostile towards Jesus' family who ran the Jerusalem mission in his time, ambivalent about the sons of Zebedee, but down on their followers if they started talking about authority. Matthew steadily exonerates both groups, and seems if anything sympathetic to the Jerusalem leadership. Luke is an irenic character, friendly to both sides. As for John, he is an ultra-Pauline. He never mentions James and John by name at all, and just refers to 'the sons of Zebedee' in the boat in 21.2. He tells us that Jesus' brothers did not believe in him (the fundamental sin in the Fourth Gospel); they tried to hustle Jesus to go to Jerusalem before his time, and Jesus said the 'world' could not hate them as it hated him. In John Jesus takes away from them their privilege of looking after his mother, and gives it to the disciple whom he loved. John's feelings were not ambivalent.

3

The Loyalty Test II: Peter

When we come to put the loyalty test to the evangelists over Peter, we find ourselves in deeper water. Peter is a favourite figure for preachers – impulsive, loyal, fallible, faithful, both-feet-in-together, all-too-human Peter. The fact is that we all *identify* with him. We hear the account of his denial the night before Good Friday, and we think, 'That might have been me!' And so the question arises about Mark's attitude to Peter: perhaps the evangelist *is* representing him as the pattern Christian, who fails in his own strength, but is forgiven through the cross and the resurrection. Surely Peter was the leader of the church, and Mark would wish to support him? And is there not a tradition that Mark was Peter's interpreter in Rome in later years?

There is indeed, and a very unreliable tradition too: it comes from Papias, bishop of Hierapolis in western Turkey about 130, and it comes alongside a series of other pieces of wishful thinking designed to defend the Gospels against those who pointed out contradictions between them. A little earlier the author of I Peter (who was not St Peter) ends his letter: 'She who is at Babylon (i.e. the church at Rome) . . . sends you greetings; and so does my son Mark'. Mark was a well-known figure in the Roman church, and mentioning him made it more plausible that Peter was the writer. But arguments from this kind of reference and from tradition are always perilous. The only way to find out Mark's attitude to Peter is to look carefully at what he says about him, and compare it with the other accounts we have. All arguments of the form, Surely Mark would have . . . , prejudge the issue. We need to look fairly at the evidence; and as before, to try to forget for the moment our interest in what Peter was actually like, and to concentrate on what Mark (and the others) thought about him. For this purpose we must certainly note all the positive stories Mark includes about him, which are for the most part the same incidents I have mentioned with James and John. But there are two passages which are about Peter on his own, and these are instructive. We may see Mark's emphasis most easily by taking another account alongside.

Here is Mark's account of 'Peter's Confession' (Mark 8.29–33):

And he asked them, But who do you say that I am? Peter answered him, You are the Christ. And he charged them to tell no one about him. And he began to teach them that the Son of Man must suffer many things . . . And he said this plainly. And Peter took him, and began to rebuke him. But turning and seeing his disciples, he rebuked Peter and said, Get behind me, Satan! For you are not on the side of God but of men.

Here is Matthew's account of the same incident (16.15–23): I have put Matthew's additions in italics:

He said to them, But who do you say that I am? *Simon* Peter replied, You are the Christ, *the Son of the living God. And Jesus answered him, Blessed are you, Simon Bar-Jona! For flesh and blood has not revealed this to you, but my Father who is in heaven. And I tell you, You are Peter, and on this rock* (Greek *petra*) *I will build my church, and the gates of Hades shall not prevail against it. I will give you the keys of the kingdom of heaven, and whatever you bind on earth shall be bound in heaven, and whatever you loose on earth shall be loosed in heaven. Then* he *commanded* them to tell no one *that he was the Christ. From that time Jesus* began to *show his disciples* that he must *go to Jerusalem and* suffer many things . . . And Peter took, and began to rebuke him, *saying, God forbid, Lord! This shall never happen to you.* But he turned *and said to* Peter, Get behind me, Satan. *You are a stumbling-block to me*; for you are not on the side of God but of men.

It is clear that Peter was the first to hail Jesus as 'the Christ' (the long promised king of the line of David – see below ch. 14); and that this was a big moment, and greatly to his credit in the eyes of all

Christians, Mark included. But a comparison of the two texts above shows how enthusiastic Matthew is about it, and how grudging is Mark. (1) In Mark Peter gives Jesus the *merely human title* 'Christ'. But Mark thought that the real significance of Jesus was that he was *divine*, 'the Son of God' (ch. 14); it is Matthew who adds 'the Son of the living God'. (2) In Mark Peter gets absolutely *no credit* for his great moment of insight; the response is chilling, like a schoolchild who feels he has written a marvellous essay and the teacher makes no comment at all. Contrast Matthew: *Blessed . . . revealed . . . Peter . . . this rock . . . the gates of Hades . . . the keys of the kingdom.* We begin to see reasons for thinking that Matthew is a Petrine. (3) Mark makes it clear that Peter has only begun on the road to understanding. He has not taken in that Jesus has to suffer, die and rise again, which are crucial to a true understanding. Matthew has this too, but he separates it from Peter's scene of triumph with 'From that time . . .'

Mark seems even to take the offensive against Peter. (4) Although Jesus explained things *plainly*, Mark says Peter had the gall to *rebuke* him – to rebuke the Son of God! Matthew makes the rebuke ever so gentle – 'God forbid, Lord!' – so gentle that it is hardly a rebuke at all. (5) This causes *Jesus to rebuke Peter*, calling him Satan, which is a pretty stinging remark; and he does it *publicly*, 'turning and seeing his disciples'. Matthew drops the latter; he retains the famous 'Satan' saying, but lets it down to mean that Peter is not only the *rock* on which the church is built, but also a rock which has nearly tripped Jesus up. (6) There is a worse matter, which is often not noticed. Jesus goes on immediately in Mark: 'If any man would come after me, let him deny himself and take up his cross and follow me. For whoever would save his life shall lose it . . .' Can you think of anyone in the Gospel story who wanted to *save his life*, who refused to *come after* Jesus and *take up his cross*, who did not *deny himself* but denied Jesus? Well, so could St Mark.

It would be an exaggeration to say that Mark was hostile to Peter in the way that he is to Jesus' family; but he is unenthusiastic, and he is determined not to allow Jerusalem Christians of his day to glorify Peter as a plaster saint over against his own hero Paul. We may see this again by contrasting his merciless treatment of Peter on Passover night with the whitewashing given by the kindly Luke (Mark 14/ Luke 22).

Peter said to him, Even though they all fall away, I will not . . . he said, vehemently, If I must die with you, I will not deny you (Mark 14.30f.).

Simon, Simon, behold, Satan demanded to have you all that he might shift you all as wheat, but I have prayed for *you* that your faith may not fail; and when you have turned again, strengthen your brethren. And he said to him, Lord, I am ready to go with you to prison and to death (Luke 22.31ff.).

Luke brings in the whole supernatural dimension. It was not just a human Peter boasting and then failing: he was up against the devil, who asked God to have him to test, as in the book of Job – which of us can withstand him? But through Jesus' prayer Peter's faith did not fail (well, it only failed for a few minutes); and later, in Acts 1–5 he strengthened his brethren in a heroic manner. Notice too the change in Peter's boast: he said he was ready to go with Jesus to prison, and he did in Acts 12 – and to death, and in the end he was martyred. It shows what you can do with an uncomfortable tradition if you try.

In Gethsemane, similarly, Mark has Jesus take Peter, James and John, and asks them to watch with him. He is very distressed, and when he comes back he says to Peter, Simon, are you asleep?; and three times he comes and they are sleeping ('for their eyes were very heavy') (Mark 14.33–42). In Luke Jesus merely tells 'the disciples' to pray, and he comes only once to find them asleep. When he does, they were asleep 'for sorrow'; isn't that touching? Peter, James and John receive an honourable non-mention; 'Simon' is not addressed. Or again, in the High Priest's courtyard, Mark has Peter deny Jesus three times, the third time with a curse on himself and an oath: Luke drops anything more than 'he said'. Mark has the cock crow twice, Luke (and Matthew) only once. Mark ends the story with the brief comment, 'and as he realized, he began to weep'. Luke means to bring out Peter's penitence: 'And the Lord turned and looked at Peter, And Peter remembered . . . and he went out and wept bitterly.'

As we go through the topics which divided the two missions, I shall have occasion often to return to Mark's unsympathetic attitude to Peter and the other pillars, and to 'the disciples' in general. But I have said enough to show which way the wind is blowing, and it may be helpful here to offer a scenario of Mark's life. In this sort of area we cannot be said to *know* anything, or even to be very confident, but we have some evidence, and we can put it together into a picture which may be something like history.

In the early 60s Paul wrote to Philemon from prison: 'Epaphras, my fellow prisoner in Christ Jesus, sends greetings to you, and so do Mark, Aristarchus, Demas and Luke, my fellow workers' (24). At the same time he (probably) wrote to the Colossians: 'Aristarchus my fellow prisoner greets you, and Mark the cousin of Barnabas . . . and Jesus who is called Justus. These are the only men of the circumcision among my fellow workers' (4.10f.). Epaphras, Luke and Demas, who were not Jews, are mentioned in the following verses. Now we hear of a 'John' (Acts 13.5, 13), who is later 'John called Mark' (15.37) and then 'Mark' (15.39). He accompanies Paul and Barnabas on the first missionary journey, but gives up after Cyprus; Barnabas wants to take him on a second mission, but Paul refuses, and he goes with Barnabas, again to Cyprus. Further, when Peter is released from prison in Acts 12, he comes to 'the house of Mary, the mother of John whose other name was Mark' (12.12). So we may think that the Jerusalem church met in the house of Mary, Mark's mother, and it will be there that in youth he knew the pillars, and heard the great stories of their share in the Lord's ministry. As a relation of Barnabas he was taken on the Cyprus mission and got to know Paul. Although he was a disappointment at first, he saw that Paul's radical policy was the way forward, and joined him in Rome (or perhaps earlier). In this way the little pieces of biographical evidence we have fit in well with the evidence of his Gospel. He knows the traditions about the disciples, and especially the Three, because they used to meet in his home; and he tells these stories with an edge on them because he ended up as a convinced disciple of Paul, their *bête noire*.

We do not have any biographical evidence about Matthew: he is certainly *not* the apostle Matthew, because his versions of the stories about Jesus are just Mark's versions with some improvements of style and theology – sometimes word for word, and even in the story of the Call of Matthew! But we can learn a lot from the changes he makes to Mark; and one of his motives in writing is likely to be his feeling that Mark had not been fair to the Jerusalem leadership.

We shall often find that where Mark is a radical, Matthew is a conservative.

What about Peter in John's Gospel? Here is John's account of Peter's Call:

> One of the two [who were Jesus' first disciples] was Andrew, Simon Peter's brother. He first found his brother Simon, and said to him, We have found the Messiah (which means Christ). He brought him to Jesus. Jesus looked at him, and said, So you are Simon the son of John? You shall be called Cephas (which means Peter) (John 1.40–42).

The reader feels disappointed, especially the reader of Matthew. Surely Peter was the *first* to be called, with Andrew; but here he is down to no. 3, and furthermore not even *called* by Jesus, just brought by Andrew to the Lord. Then in Matthew it was *Peter* who realized that Jesus was the Messiah, and Jesus said that flesh and blood had not revealed this to him; but here it seems that *his own* flesh and blood revealed it to him, his own brother! Finally, where is the thrill, the moment of triumph in Jesus' voice which rings out so clearly in the Matthew account above? It is dissolved into the flat, unexcited, unexplained naming as John describes it.

This disappointment is a harbinger of things to come. In the Synoptics Peter was the spokesman for the Twelve; in John he is hardly mentioned through the ministry (John 1–12), and the spokesmen are Philip, Andrew and Thomas. In place of Peter's high insight, 'You are the Christ', all he can rise to in John is 'we have believed, and have come to know, that you are the Holy One of God' (6.69). This was the limit that Jerusalem Christianity would go to (see ch. 14). At the Last Supper Peter makes a goat of himself (13.2–11). At first he will not let Jesus wash his feet – 'Lord, do you wash my feet? . . . You shall never wash my feet'. Jesus has to explain that what he is doing is a profound mystery – 'What I am doing you do not know now, but afterward you will understand . . . If I do not wash you you have no part with me'. In other words the washing is the equivalent of baptism. But Peter gets hold of the wrong end of the stick, and now wants 'not my feet only but also my hands and my head'! A little later the disciple who cuts off the High priest's servant's ear, who has been anonymous in the other Gospels, becomes Peter in John (18.10f.).

An important novel feature in John is the appearance of a new character, 'the disciple whom Jesus loved' (i.e. Jesus' favourite disciple), who first appears at the Last Supper. He is never named, and has been a puzzle to many; it used to be thought that he was St John the apostle, but this idea has now been virtually given up. We may think of him as the founder of John's church, for he is in every way a hero, and he constantly puts Peter in the shade. It is he who is lying in Jesus' bosom at the Supper, and Peter has to ask through him whom Jesus means as the traitor (13.23–26). He knows the High Priest personally, and gets Peter past the checkpoint into the courtyard (18.15f.). He stands faithfully by the cross when Peter is away nursing a sore conscience (19.26f.). He outruns Peter to the tomb, and is the first to believe in the resurrection (20.2–10). He recognizes Jesus from the boat, and tells Peter it is the Lord (21.7). Peter is humbled by Jesus' triple questioning whether he loves him, and is promised the high calling of martyrdom; but the Beloved Disciple is to be Jesus' permanent witness, until he comes. Peter asks, 'Lord, what about this man?', and is told, 'If it is my will that he remain until I come, what is it to you? Follow me': mind your own business, Peter.

It is often dismaying to those who have read the Bible for spiritual edification to find what appears to be a series of character assassinations. But I think it is a mistake to be too distressed. No movement as vital as the early church could fail to feel strongly the importance of the principles that were at stake. We have already seen James and Peter take their stand on observing the Law of God, while Paul saw the admission of the Gentiles on practicable terms as God's command. These were noble aspirations, to be upheld by advancing or diminishing the reputations of their respective champions. By John's time the issue was even more crucial: the truth or otherwise of the claim that Jesus was the eternal Word of God. For such credal certainties, and the power that goes with them, later movements were to sink to real assassinations, like that of Trotsky; and the Catholic Church was to burn dissidents alive by the hundred. By such standards the strategies of St Mark and St John were gentlemanly.

Even Dr Johnson thought that when a man engages in controversy for the faith, 'he is to do all he can to lessen his antagonist, because authority from personal respect has much weight with most people, and often more than reasoning' (1776).

4

Meat, Wine and Sabbath

Being a Jew was in many ways a simple matter; you were born into a community which knew and provided for Jewish ways. Becoming a Christian in the early years of the church was not so easy; for Christianity was not an independent religion at all, but a sub-division of Judaism. In Paul's lifetime almost all Christians were Jews; the leadership was in Jerusalem; the accepted authority was the Jewish scriptures, our Old Testament. For a non-Jewish convert this meant various problems, of which the two most immediate arose over meat and the sabbath, in rather different ways.

The law about meat was in the book of Leviticus: 'No person among you shall eat blood . . . for the life of all flesh, its blood is in its life' (Lev. 17.12–14). The life of the animal was thought of as ebbing away as its blood poured out; and this mysterious element 'life' was felt to be holy, and to belong to God. From a practical point of view, however, this did not tell the butcher too much. He knew he must cut the animal's throat, but *how* and *how much* blood must run away? So the Jewish sages, the Wise, as they were called, developed rules about where the knife must be put in to stop the animal choking to death, how much washing was necessary, etc. These rules were discussed by scripture experts (*doreshim*), and were put about by the 'scribes' who acted as village schoolmasters and local authorities on tradition. The result was *kosher* meat, which was available everywhere in Palestine, and there were *kosher* butchers in every Jewish community abroad.

When Paul preached in a town, it was a matter of luck how this affected the new church. The converts needed somewhere to meet, and that meant the house of somebody of independent means; and there might be only one or two such people. Paul used to preach in the synagogue, and he might convert a well-to-do Jew, in which case there would be no problem. But sometimes, as at Antioch, the church's host was a Gentile; and when the Christians met, on Saturday evenings, he would provide the supper. Well-to-do people ate meat, and generous hosts would provide meat for the church; and one cannot very easily say to one's host, 'Excuse me, before I touch this, is it *kosher*?' Well you *can*, but it rather spoils the atmosphere, and Paul would not do so.

We have seen (ch. 1) that 'those of James' pushed Peter into asking this question in Antioch (Gal. 2.11–14); and this raises the question of how Paul had handled the problem before, and what arrangement had been made in the Jerusalem conference of Gal. 2.1–10. This becomes clear from an earlier letter of Paul's, I Corinthians. Greek people were great admirers of wisdom; they had invented philosophy, which means the love of wisdom. So when Jewish people settled among them, they presented their religion as the highest wisdom, with texts like 'The fear of the Lord is the beginning of wisdom'. Wisdom was embodied in the Law (Ecclus. 24), and when Christian missionaries from Jerusalem arrived in Corinth, they impressed Paul's Gentile converts with their wisdom, and with the way in which many detailed rules could be derived from the text of the Law.

Paul is worried by this, and quotes Isaiah, 'I will destroy the wisdom of the Wise'. He asks, 'Where is the Sage? where is the scribe? where is the scripture expert of this age? Has not God made foolish the wisdom of the world?' (I Cor. 1.19f.). He makes it clear that he is behind the Law of God itself, but that he rejects the detailed rules made by the learned. He writes 'that your faith might not rest in the wisdom of men . . . we impart this not in taught words of human wisdom' (2.5,13). The principle which they are to learn from him and his friend Apollos is 'Not beyond what is written' (4.6) – i.e. the Bible and the Bible only. So, in other words, Christians do not have to worry if the beef at the eucharistic supper is *kosher* or not; that is *taught* words of *human* wisdom. All they have to do is to be sure that the bull's throat was cut; but then all butchers cut the bull's throat. Strangling bulls is a rare enterprise.

Paul does not tell us what he said to the Pillars at Jerusalem; only that 'they imposed nothing on me' (Gal. 2.6). He will have assured them that he insisted on no idolatry, on sexual purity, etc.; and if they asked about meat, he could say, 'We keep the Law'. Luke gives a somewhat inflated account of the same incident in Acts 15: what had been a private meeting has become a Council approaching the size of Vatican II. But the 'decree' issued at the end of the meeting is probably roughly what was agreed: 'That you abstain from what has been sacrificed to idols, and from blood, and from what is strangled, and from unchastity' (Acts 15.29). It was well-known among Jews that no Gentile could resist going into an idol-temple or a whorehouse; so that was agreed with Paul's full concurrence. The law about blood was no problem if one stuck to Leviticus, and the prohibition of strangling just made it clear that no more detailed ruling about *kosher* meat was involved. The only thing that mattered was that the animal's throat had been slit: *not beyond what is written*, the Bible and the Bible only.

The issue over meat was the first to crop up because that involved the *Jewish* members of the church: they did not want to become Law-breakers ('sinnners'), so they wanted to be clear that if they ate meat at the eucharist it was not tainted. Paul's distinction between the God-given Bible and the *taught words of human wisdom* was useful here, but it was not so good when it came to the second issue, the sabbath. For unfortunately the sabbath law is in the Bible – in fact it is the Fourth Commandment: 'Remember the sabbath day to keep it holy. Six days you shall labour, and do all your work; but the seventh day is a sabbath to the LORD your God; in it you shall not do any work'. Paul could not say that the sabbath law was a taught word of human wisdom.

Keeping sabbath was not difficult for Jews, and the day's holiday was much valued, and was a public symbol of Jewishness. Jewish people were clannish, and if a young Jew came to Rome or somewhere, he had the address of a cousin who could give him a roof and see him into a job, working for another Jew. The Jewish firm would keep sabbath, as the brothers Reichmann kept sabbath in the modern property company Olympia and York; and all the employees would stop work from Friday sundown. But what about a newly converted Christian, working for a pagan employer, perhaps the Imperial civil service? What would be the result if he said, 'I've become a Christian, sir, so I'm afraid I won't be able to come in to work tomorrow'? Most employers would say, 'All right; and don't come in on Sunday either

– you're fired'. Christians did not expect to have to starve; so they felt that the sabbath law did not apply to them – and Paul could not but sympathize.

The two issues came up together in the Roman church, and caused Paul to write Romans. There had been a riot in Rome in 49. The Roman historian Suetonius says it was started by a man called Chrestus (*Claudius*, 25.4); and this is probably a misunderstanding for Chrestus (which would be pronounced the same). Some Jews (at least) were expelled from Rome, including the Jewish Christian Aquila (Acts 18.2); and very likely most Jewish Christians had to leave. When they came back, they found Gentile Christians running the church, and not keeping to Jewish ways. Paul writes:

As for the man who is weak in the faith, welcome him, but not for disputes over opinions. One believes he may eat anything, while the weak man eats only vegetables. Let not him who eats despise him who abstains, and let not him who abstains pass judgment on him who eats; for God has welcomed him . . . One man esteems one day as better than another, while another man esteems all days alike. Let everyone be fully convinced in his own mind. He who observes the day, observes it in honour of the Lord. He also who eats, eats in honour of the Lord, since he gives thanks to God; while he who abstains, abstains in honour of the Lord and gives thanks to God. None of us lives to himself, and none of us dies to himself (Rom. 14.1–8).

The established members of the church are to welcome those *weak in the faith*, that is the Jewish Christians; but *not for disputes over opinions* – the Jewish Christian incomers are not to wreck the peace of the church by insisting on their views. The Gentile Christians have been eating non-kosher meat, and the Jewish Christians will not touch this and *eat only vegetables*. Also the Gentile Christians have to work on Saturdays, and are said to *esteem all days alike*; while the Jewish Christians *observe the day*, that is the sabbath, because they work for Jewish employers who give them Saturdays off. There is a bit of an 'atmosphere' in the church. The Gentiles *despise* the Jewish Christians for being legalistic, pettifogging, etc., while the Jewish Christians *pass judgment* on the Gentiles as Law-breakers and sinners.

As the Jewish group had to make do with bread and cabbage, to the aroma of mutton hot-pot being enjoyed by the non-Jews, it is not difficult to imagine the jolly time that was had by all.

Paul thinks to pour oil on these troubled waters in two ways. First, in the passage set out above, he gives authority to personal conscience. *Let everyone be fully convinced in his own mind.* (This is a popular resource even today, and a most dangerous one: the Broederbond in South Africa are *fully convinced* of the virtue of apartheid.) This is then followed by some good rhetoric: *None of us lives to himself,* etc. So far the Gentile Christians (Paulines) have in fact won the day; for they have permission to disregard the Law if their conscience tells them to, and it does. However, in a second move Paul insists on the duty of love, of not making one's brother stumble: 'Everything is indeed clean, but it is wrong for anyone to make others fall by what he eats' (14.20). He knows that in fact Jewish Christians (Petrines) will stop coming to church if they have to share the eucharist with a lot of 'sinners' eating tainted meat while they have to go vegetarian and are despised for it. So it is not so surprising that he put together sixteen chapters of complex argument in the frail hope of keeping the church together. He stood about as much chance as Canute did with the tide.

The same problems recur in other churches than Rome. In Galatia we met the meat problem at 2.12: at 4.10 Paul says, 'You observe days, and months, and seasons, and years! I am afraid I have laboured over you in vain' – *days,* that is sabbaths; *months,* that is new moons; *seasons,* that is the cycle of festivals and fasts; *years,* that is the whole Jewish calendar. In Colosse it was the same: 'let no one pass judgment on you in questions of food and drink, or with regard to a festival or a new moon or a sabbath' (Col. 2.16). It is the same *passing judgment* that we had in Rom. 14, and the same calendar (now plainly Jewish with *new moon* and *sabbath*); and food and drink mean meat and wine as in Rom. 14 too. Jews would not drink uncertified wine, for fear that a cup of it had been poured out as a libation to a pagan god. But we do not hear so much about making brethren stumble now. These are churches in Turkey founded by Paulines and now being re-evangelized by a Petrine counter-mission; and there must be some limit to charity.

With time charity faded, as the Paulines grew in numbers and in confidence. Mark tells how Jesus ate at the table of sinners, like the tax-collector Levi, and the Pharisees criticized him for it (Mark 2.15–17); rather as James and the others criticized Paul for eating non-kosher meat with Gentiles ('Gentile sinners', as Paul himself calls them, Gal. 2.15). Mark says Jesus' comment was, 'Those who are well have no need of a physician, but those who are sick; I came not to call the righteous, but sinners'. He comes back to the question of defilement in 7.14–23. Jesus says categorically, 'there is nothing outside a man which by going into him can defile him; but the things which come out of a man are what defile him' (7.15). This virtually abolishes the whole *kosher* system (*kashrut*); and that is how Mark understands it, for he adds, 'Thus he declared all foods clean' (7.19) – which would justify the Pauline practice at the eucharist, with non-kosher meat provided by a Gentile host. So it would appear from Mark that, so far as meat was concerned, Jesus was a Pauline; only it did not worry Mark if the Petrine brethren did stumble – more fools them.

Jesus was a Pauline in the Marcan sabbath stories too. In Mark 2.23–28 the disciples are plucking corn on the sabbath, and the Pharisees again start criticizing. Jesus appeals to the example of David who overrode ceremonial rules about the shewbread when he was hungry; and concludes, 'The sabbath was made for man, not man for the sabbath; so the Son of Man is lord even of the sabbath' (2.27f.). In other words, Jesus has authority to repeal the Fourth Commandment, according to Mark; and Christians do not have to observe it unless it is convenient. What a happy saying for a Pauline! In the following story Jesus heals a man with a withered hand on the sabbath, and the Pharisees first criticize and then plot Jesus' death (3.1–6). This time Jesus' punch-line is, 'Is it lawful on the sabbath to do good or to do harm, to save life or to kill?' The hearer is left in no doubt of the moral. Pharisees observe sabbath and plot murder on it; (Pauline) Christians observe it *in spirit* by doing good on it. The issue of whether one should actually *work* on it is left conveniently vague.

When we turn to Matthew, we can see a Petrine revising these dangerous comments. The most perilous is Mark 2.27, 'The sabbath was made for man . . .', because that is an open invitation to sabbath-breaking, and Matthew cannot countenance that. So he leaves it out (Matt. 12.1–8); and so does Luke (Luke 6.1–5). Of course Jewish tradition always ruled that human need took priority over sabbath, so Matthew stresses that the disciples *were hungry* – poor chaps, they had not eaten for a fortnight. Actually Matthew was very keen on the sabbath. Mark tells the Christians to pray that when they flee to the mountains it may not be in the winter; Matthew adds 'or on a sabbath' (24.20), for a good Matthaean Christian will not go more than a sabbath day's journey even with the Great Tribulation advancing behind him. Similarly Matthew leaves out Mark's comment 'Thus he declared all food clean', and turns the discussion about defilement into a contrast between various evil thoughts and hand-washing: 'These are what defile a man; but to eat with unwashed hands does not defile a man' (15.20).

At first sight, these Gospel stories raise no problem. Jesus was, it seems to Mark, a radical; and Paul simply inherited his radical views, and applied them to the Gentile mission. But then how are we to explain the attitude of Peter and the other Pillars? They had heard Jesus say all these things, and yet they *opposed* Paul's radical policies; they had been entrusted with Jesus' message, yet they were solid conservatives. Also we have the difficulty that Paul is doing his best to win the argument for radicalism, and he knows a number of Jesus' sayings, but *he never appeals to any radical saying of Jesus*. Why not? There are also other problems. It would be very difficult for any Jewish religious teacher to gain a wide following if he said he was repealing the Law of God; and problems about *kosher* meat and sabbath only really arose for Gentiles.

So it seems simpler to take the matter the other way round. Paul had to fight for the principles that *all food is clean* and that *the sabbath is made for man*. Mark was a Pauline, and he reshaped stories of Jesus' disputes with Pharisees to turn Jesus into a true-pink Pauline. We know that James was close to Pharisees in Jerusalem from Josephus (*Antiquities*, 20.9.1) and Hegesippus (Eusebius, *Ecclesiastical History* 2.23), so the constant Pharisaic criticism fits in conveniently. But actually Jesus was a conservative about the Law, a pious Jew; his radicalism was about the kingdom. Peter and the others were faithful to their master's teaching, and knew that Paul was making alarming innovations. Matthew did his best to reinstate Jesus' conservative image; he subtly reshaped the Marcan stories, and we hardly notice his brilliant handiwork.

5

The Whole Law

The meat issue came up first because that involved the Jewish Christians in 'sinning'; then sabbath and the calendar because these were public badges of observing, or of defying the Law. Circumcision was not an issue at first. It was not a public matter; you could not tell by looking at a man in church if he had been circumcised. It did not apply to the women. In any case, in synagogues all over the Empire Gentile 'God-fearers' were accepted without circumcision, rather in the way that 'attenders' are at Quaker meetings. People might take time to commit themselves finally, and it may be rather off-putting if the sidesman says to you as he hands you the hymn-book, 'Welcome to St Mary's – have you been circumcised? Just go through the door on the left'. So when Paul and Barnabas went up to sort things out with the Pillars, Titus 'was not compelled to be circumcised' (Gal. 2.3).

But of course circumcision is required by the Law, both for natural-born Jews and for those who opt to join the people of God (Gen. 17.9–14; Ex. 12.48f.); and sooner or later the Petrines knew the issue would have to be faced. Jewish Christians were committed to keeping the whole Law of God *and more*; Gentile men who joined the people of God must do so by getting circumcised, and then they could keep the whole of God's Law and more. The matter is put with dramatic simplicity by that good Petrine St Matthew:

Think not that I have come to abolish the law and the prophets; I have come not to abolish them, but to fulfil them. For truly I say to you, till heaven and earth pass away, not an iota, not a dot, will pass from the law, until all is accomplished. Whoever then relaxes one of the least of these commandments and teaches men so, shall be called least in the kingdom of heaven; but he who does them and teaches them shall be called great in the kingdom of heaven. For I tell you, unless your righteousness exceeds that of the scribes and Pharisees, you will never enter the kingdom of heaven. (Matt. 5.17–20).

Matthew is a marvellous teacher: he makes everything so clear. Disciples of Paul like Mark are a serious menace, suggesting that the food-laws have been abrogated, or the Fourth Commandment repealed. Nothing of the kind: the whole *Law and the Prophets* are valid, every *iota* (the smallest Greek letter, every *yod*, the smallest Hebrew letter), every crown on a letter, and they are valid *till heaven and earth pass away, till all is accomplished*. So teachers like Mark who go about *relaxing* even *the least commandment* (let alone the Ten Commandments!), and *teaching men so* in their Gospels, can hardly expect to go to heaven even; while people like Peter and James who have stood up for the validity of God's Law will be honoured there. The basis of religion is given by God in the first five books of the Bible, and of course this has to be kept. But on its own that is not enough – the *scribes and Pharisees*, the Jewish leadership of the 70s when Matthew was writing – do that. Christians do more, they do the *fulfilment* of the Law. For instance, the Law said, 'You shall not murder'; but Christians must not even be angry, because anger is a kind of murder in one's heart. The Law said, 'You shall not commit adultery'; but Christians must not even think of a woman in the wrong sort of way, because that is adultery in the heart. Christianity is a higher *righteousness*, the *fulfilment of the Law*, the quest for *perfection* (5.21–48).

Matthew's religion is a noble aspiration, a rigorously honest acceptance of the conditions divinely laid down in scripture, and beyond. Scripture covers in the main the *actions* required of us; the Lord required more, the *dispositions* of the heart. Matthew had a poetic gift which was able to enshrine these teachings in peerless eloquence; and no one who reads his Sermon on the Mount can fail to be attracted by its will to selflessness – *Be therefore perfect*. This is the stuff that sent men with first-class degrees to be slum-priests and debutantes into the convent. We cannot be surprised if Petrines, used to an appeal like this, despised the response of the Paulines as a string of hypocrisies.

We have already seen the Pauline dilemma over meat and the sabbath; but Paul and his followers were obliged to defend their stand over the fundamental principle of the Law. They were in an impossible position because they believed two contradictory things. They thought the Law was God's Law, and that Gentiles should not murder, fornicate, etc.; but they knew that if they required sabbath observance, circumcision, etc., which were equally part of the Law, that would be the end of the Gentile mission. So they were reduced to offering a series of arguments which were weak and self-contradictory. I mention some of them here, but the list is not intended to be exhaustive.

1. *We keep the biblical Law, but not the oral interpretations of it.* I have already alluded to this approach (ch. 4), which is set out in I Cor. 1–4 with the contrast between *taught words of human wisdom* and *Not beyond what is written.* Paul cited Isa. 29.14, 'I will destroy the wisdom of the wise . . .', but he has also in mind Isa. 29.13, 'This people draw near with their mouth . . . while their heart is far from me, *teaching* as doctrines the precepts *of men.*' This argument was useless once one left issues like *kosher* meat, because many central matters (like sabbath and circumcision) *were written* in the Bible. Nor is it any use having a law if no one knows how it is to be applied. But Paul himself continued to use this line to the end of his life. He says to the Colossians, 'Why do you submit to regulations (Greek *dogmatizesthe*), Do not handle, do not touch, do not taste, . . . according to *the doctrines and precepts of men*?' (2.20ff.). In Eph. 2.15 Christ is said to have broken down the law of commandments *in regulations* (Greek *dogmasin*): Paul is constantly quoting the Bible in Ephesians to support his ethical exhortations – it is not the *Bible* which Christ has broken down by the cross, but the regulations which the sages derived from it.

A good slogan goes much further than a decent argument, and Mark takes up the baton. Some Pharisees came from Jerusalem, he says, and saw that some of the disciples did not wash their hands before eating; so they asked Jesus why his followers did not follow the tradition of the elders. Jesus then replies, 'Well did Isaiah prophesy of you hypocrites, as it is written, This people honours me with their lips . . . teaching *as doctrines the precepts of men*' (7.1–8; Isa. 29.13). The discussion soon moves on from *washing before* eating to *what one may eat*, since the Pharisees thought both *defiled* one; and Mark's Pauline congregation will have greatly enjoyed hearing not only that Jesus said all food was clean, but also that anyone who disagreed was a hypocrite, condemned by divine authority in Isaiah. They probably also remembered that the Jewish Christians who criticized them were *Pharisees* from *Jerusalem*.

Honest Matthew does not blink the problem. No Law is any good unless we know how to apply it – does running an Olympic heat count as work? Is Sunday now the sabbath? He writes: 'The scribes and Pharisees sit on Moses' seat; so practise and observe whatever they tell you' (23.2); 'you tithe mint and anice and cummin, and have neglected the weightier matters of the law, justice and mercy and faith; these you ought to have done, without neglecting the others' (23.23). Judaism provided a tradition for interpreting the Law: earlier the sages, by Matthew's time the Pharisaic party which took over Judaism after the destruction of Jerusalem in 70. These learned men are said to *sit on Moses' seat*; and Christians (rather to the surprise of some modern readers) are to *practise and observe whatever they tell you*. In rough terms this might mean keeping the regulations laid down in the Mishnah, whose English translation is available with about 800 pages of rulings. This work tells you what to do with any mint, anice or cummin you may be growing. Justice and mercy may be more important laws, but *tithing* these is *not to be neglected*, and the vicar will be very impressed as you bring them to church for the Harvest Festival.

2. *Abraham was justified (reckoned to be righteous) by his faith, and the Law was given only later.* At the Jerusalem conference in 48 the Pillars had played softly, softly, on the circumcision issue; but by the middle 50s it was clear that this would not do. They had stopped the rot at Antioch, but Paul had not only founded a string of churches in central Turkey (Galatia); there was also a line of them round the Aegean Sea, from Corinth in southern Greece (Achaea) through northern Greece (Macedonia) to Ephesus in western Turkey. So a deputation was despatched to Galatia with instructions to read the riot act: the seal of belonging to God's people was, for men, circumcision, and no man was a Christian who was not circumcised.

Fortunately for the future of the Christian church, some obstinate men in Iconium or somewhere did not fancy the knife, and wrote to ask what Paul thought about it.

One became a Christian in the primary sense by *faith*, by *believing*; and Paul was lucky enough to find a text in Genesis which echoed this. Abraham is an old man, and God promises him children; and it is said, 'And *he believed* the LORD; and it was reckoned to him as righteousness' (Gen. 15.6). Now in the first-century world, Jew and Gentile alike expected judgment by God on death; and for this purpose it was essential to be counted *righteous* and not guilty. So the Genesis text combined three elements usefully, even if the meaning had to be stretched a bit: *being reckoned righteous* comes, it seems, from *believing*, in fact from *believing God's promise*. There is no mention of any commands, or laws of God. So Paul is able to write back in Gal. 3 (and later in Rom. 4), pointing to this as the divine answer. The law was given four centuries later, and cannot affect the earlier promise (Gal. 3.17f.); even circumcision was not ordained until Gen. 17, two chapters later. So it is *faith* which brings salvation (being found *righteous* on Judgment Day), and not *works of the law* (like circumcision).

This dubious piece of logic is compounded by a series of further moves. God's promise was to Abraham 'and to your seed', i.e. his descendants; but 'seed' is singular, and Paul says that must refer to a single person, i.e. Christ (Gal. 3.16). Also there is a text in the prophets which says, in the Hebrew, 'But the righteous shall live by his faithfulness', and in the Greek, '. . . by faith in me'. Paul drops the 'his' or 'in me', and takes the words to mean that eternal life will be granted to the righteous (Christian) because of his faith (in Christ) (Gal. 3.11f.). There is also an argument about Christ becoming a curse for us which Paul wisely never used again.

Galatians 3 is not a happy chapter. It is written by a man with his back to the wall, driven to what arguments he can force out of scripture; the impression given is of a cleversticks who is bent on proving that black is white. The Petrines said of Paul that he was a scoundrel and a crook (Greek *panourgos, dolos*, II Cor. 12.16), and we can see their point. Even if Paul were justified in his claim that *salvation* is based on *faith*, the plain sense of scripture is that you should keep the Law as well. So the saint is reduced to saying that the Law was only given by angels (3.19f.) – like a speeding motorist who says that the speed limit is a police regulation. Or he says that the law *caused* sin, by suggestion (Rom. 7.7–11). But in the same breath he says that it is holy and just and good (Rom. 7.12) and that he upholds it (Rom. 3.31).

3. *The Law was our custodian; now we are adult in Christ* (Gal. 3.23–4.11). Paul uses two images: first the *paidagogos*, the slave who was given charge of the upbringing of an upper-class boy in Roman times; then the *epitropos*, the guardian who was in charge of a minor until he became of age (at fourteen). In both cases the boy is under discipline, including the birch; and readers of *Tom Jones* may remember the method by which Parson Thwackum scourged error out of Tom. So even though the boy will in time inherit the father's property, he is under a temporary, and oppressive, regimen, not different in principle from that endured by slaves. In the same way mankind has hitherto been under the Law, with punishments duly administered for any trespasses; but now that Christ has come, we are made adult sons of God, and are out of its clutches. There is a similar approach in II Cor. 3 where the Law is the old covenant, and passing away; while in Christ there has come a new covenant, of eternal glory.

This is a splendid argument, to which most modern churchmen would gladly say Amen; but then most modern churchmen do not quote the Old Testament as the basis of their morals, as Paul did.

4. The most fruitful line the Paulines developed was that *Love is the fulfilment of the Law*. It was a practice of the time to look for a summary statement of the Torah; as when a man asked the sage Hillel to teach him the Law while he stood on one leg, and Hillel gave him a negative form of the Golden Rule. So Paul says:

> he who loves his neighbour has fulfilled the Law. The commandments, You shall not commit adultery . . . , and any other commandment are summed up in this sentence, You shall love your neighbour as yourself. Love does no wrong to a neighbour; therefore love is the fulfilling of the Law (Rom. 13.8–10, citing Lev. 19.18; cf. Gal. 5.14).

This is a brilliant move. Every reader will be impressed with the neatness of taking a single principle, the highly convincing one of love, as comprising many detailed actions. But then it is not at all obvious that one needs to be circumcised in order to love one's neighbour; so the real difficulties are comfortably evaded.

Paul is doing all he can to support his Gentile converts in ignoring the circumcision Law; and it is noticeable that he does not quote Jesus' remark on this very topic. So it is likely that Mark has again done some creative embroidery in the story of the scribe who asks Jesus which is the first commandment. Jesus replies 'The first is, Hear, O Israel, the Lord our God, the Lord is one; and you shall love the Lord your God . . . The second is this, You shall love your neighbour as yourself' (Mark 12.28–34). The 'first' commandment is in fact the *Shema*', the Hear, O Israel, which Jews said three times a day, as Christians say the Lord's Prayer. Mark could not have Jesus *just* reply 'Love your neighbour', because loving God is very important in the Bible. So he puts the *Shema*' first and Lev. 19.18 second, which Paul had taught him was the essence of Christianity. Further the scribe concludes that love is much more than sacrifices; so the Marcan Christian nods comfortably – love is all, and Jewish ceremonies are out of date.

By John's time this battle is over. John has Jesus speak of 'the law of Moses' (7.23), 'your law' (10.34); it is not God's law any more, though he does not mind quoting it as a divine prophecy! Instead of the Law, we hear repeatedly of a *new commandment, that you love one another*. The instructed reader of the Old Testament is surprised, because love has an important place there; but it is new to John in the sense that it is now, as in Rom. 13, the fundamental principle of all action. It has *replaced* the Law, and that indeed is something new. It is a pity that although John is the most insistent of New Testament authors on the primacy of love, his heart is to a large extent filled with hatred of 'the Jews'; but did not the Lord say, 'practise and observe whatever they tell you, but not what they do'?

The arguments of the Paulines on the Law are a series of evasions, muddles and contradictions; but we should not view them as the Petrines did, as the work of scoundrels and crooks. Paul was a great man, seized with a great idea: that Christianity made divine salvation available to the whole of humankind. He could see that this would be frustrated if too much of the Torah was insisted upon; but he did not see that it was necessary to be even more radical, and view the Old Covenant as the word of man as well as of God. This insight would require another eighteen centuries of debate; we do well not to be too censorious.

6

The Kingdom: Already or Not Yet?

Jesus (probably) did not make many alarming innovations about the Law; he preached about the *kingdom of God* (or of *heaven*, as pious Jews like Matthew expressed it, to avoid using the name of God). For many centuries Jews had spoken of God reigning, and when he did, that would be the end of foreign tyrannies, and of poverty and disease: there would be peace and plenty for all, and Jews would run the world (Dan. 2; 7) and see that God's ways were observed. Much of Jesus' preaching was about the coming of this kingdom. In some of his sayings and parables it seems that the kingdom *has come*, and in others as if it *is going to come very soon*.

The difference is important, for reasons we shall see. Here is Paul, in high dudgeon:

> Already you are stuffed full! Already you have become rich! Without us you have begun to reign! And I wish you had begun to reign that we might share the reign with you! (I Cor. 4.8).

The repeated *Already*! is sarcastic. A group of Corinthians have gone in for a lot of unrealistic talk about the kingdom of God having arrived, and they see themselves as sharing in Christ's *reign*. This can be seen in their claims to speak with angelic tongues, to have visions, to be able to perform healings and so on (I Cor. 12); they have been *enriched* (I Cor. 1.5) with all these gifts; and furthermore, thanks to the early Christian idealism in which money was pooled, they are *stuffed full* of good food, while the wretched apostle goes *hungry and thirsty . . . working with our own hands* (I Cor. 4.11). The vacuousness of their talk makes him angry. 'I will come to you soon', he says, 'and I will find out not the talk of these arrogant people but their power. For the *kingdom of God* does not consist in talk but in power' (4.19f.). Later in the letter Paul will say, 'Flesh and blood cannot inherit the kingdom of God, nor does the perishable inherit the imperishable' (15.50). We cannot have the kingdom of God in this age: this age will come to an end when Christ returns; we shall be changed so as to have imperishable bodies, and we will enjoy the imperishable kingdom then.

Paul does not speak much of the kingdom in his letters: when he mentions the kingdom of God it is always in the future, and he is generally warning people that if they behave badly they will not inherit it (e.g. I Cor. 6.9,10). The context shows that the people who *did* talk a lot about it as having arrived were the Petrines, 'those of Cephas' in 1.12. They have been 'judging' Paul not to be a proper apostle, and have been 'puffed up for the one [leader] against the other' (4.1–6), i.e. for Peter against Paul; we have exactly the same 'judging' of Paul's apostleship compared with Peter and the others in 9.3–5. Paul has tactfully 'transposed' the issue on to himself and Apollos to get the message over (4.6). So we have the same line-up as we had over the Law. The Petrines saw the kingdom as having arrived *already*; the Paulines thought it was still to come.

As with the Law issue, the problem over the kingdom spills over into the Gospels. John, whom we have found to be more Pauline than Paul on other points, is the same here. There is only one passage in the whole Gospel where the kingdom of God is spoken of, and there it is negative. Jesus says to Nicodemus, 'Truly, truly, I say to you, unless one is born anew, he cannot see the kingdom of God . . . unless one is born of water and the Spirit, he cannot enter the kingdom of God' (John 3.3,5). Nicodemus is – in John's mind – an unpleasing character: a Pharisee, a ruler of the Jews (the very groups which most opposed Jesus' work), he comes to Jesus by night (because he is afraid to be seen consorting with Jesus) with the greasy gambit, 'Rabbi, we know that you are a teacher come from God' (cf. Matt. 22.16). But his faith is based on signs, a most inadequate foundation for true religion (cf. 4.48), and typical of Jewish Christians (I Cor. 1.22); he has not even begun on the spiritual life, and needs to be *born anew*. His questions to Jesus show him to be spiritually empty (cf. 3.10,12). He is, to John, the pattern Jewish Christian half-believer, talking about the *kingdom of God*, but without the faith to *see* it, let alone *enter* it. What he needs is a totally new spiritual start, symbolized by the *water and Spirit* of baptism. The kingdom gets short shrift in John.

Mark is also a Pauline, and again the kingdom is a future thing for him, and mostly spoken of in the negative. Jesus' first preaching proclaims, 'The time is fulfilled, and the kingdom of God is at hand; repent and believe in the gospel' (Mark 1.15). It is not here yet; it *is at hand* (Greek *engiken*) it has drawn near. At 9.1 Jesus will say, 'Truly, I say to you, there are some standing here who will not taste death before they see the kingdom of God having come in power'. Mark, like all early Christians, was expecting the end of the age soon; and in this case he is specific. *Some standing here*, say in AD 30, *will not have tasted death*, will not be dead, *before they see the kingdom come in power*. Matthew makes that even clearer by rephrasing, 'before they see the Son of Man coming in his kingdom' (Matt. 16.28). In other words Jesus' Return was expected in the lifetime of some of his hearers, or in rough terms before 90: *that* would be when the kingdom of God would begin. Notice Mark's phrase *in power*, echoing Paul's in I Cor. 4.20. What we have now is *talk*; what we are looking for is *power*, when we will look out of the door and not see beggars starving and Roman soldiers driving Jews off in slavery. Mark makes the same point at 13.30. He has given a conspectus of things to come, leading up to the coming of the Son of Man from heaven (13.26); and he ends, 'Truly, I say to you, this generation will not pass away before all these things take place'. *This generation* is the same as *some standing here* in 9.1. Mark was writing in about 70, and he probably did not live to see his hopes disappointed.

Mark features the kingdom in a number of sayings, where again the future association is unmistakable. John is warned (see ch. 2) that it is better to enter life maimed rather than with two hands to go to Gehenna (hell); and then that it is better to enter the kingdom of God with one eye rather than with two eyes to be thrown into Gehenna (9.43,47). Here *entering the kingdom of God* is the same as *entering life*; and both of these, and the alternative to them, are what happen to us at Judgment Day, with Christ's Coming. Jesus says to the disciples, 'How hard will it be for those who have riches to enter the kingdom of God' (10.23). Peter, by contrast, has left everything for Jesus, and he is promised a hundred times all that he has given up 'now in this time . . . and in the age to come eternal life' (10.29f.). *Entering the kingdom* and having *eternal life* are both future things, they *will be, in the age to come.*

Matthew, on the other hand, we have found to be a Petrine; and unsurprisingly we find in his Gospel a number of sayings which speak of the kingdom as having come already. Jesus has been casting out some demons, and has been criticized as doing this by Beelzebul, the prince of demons. He replies, 'But if it is by the Spirit of God that I cast out demons, then the kingdom of God has come upon you' (12.28). According to this, Jesus' exorcizing power was a proof that *the kingdom of God has come.* Matthew speaks of the *kingdom of God*, rather than *of heaven*, because of the contrast with *Satan's kingdom* in 12.26. Similarly in Matt. 11 John has been imprisoned, and sends to ask if Jesus is the promised one. Jesus points to his healings, and then praises John, including the comment: 'From the days of John the Baptist until now the kingdom of heaven has suffered violence, and men of violence rape it' (11.14). *From the days of John the Baptist until now* comprises the period covered between Matt. 3, when John begins preaching, and Matt. 11. In that time John has been arrested and put in prison where he will be executed; and Jesus has been constantly harried by carping Pharisees and others, who in the end will execute him. These are *men of violence*, and they are *raping* the kingdom of heaven, that is the earthly John-Jesus movement which we may speak of as the embryo church. *The kingdom of heaven* is thus a *present entity*, a movement of real people in the present world, which is under constant attack by *men of violence*. So for Matthew the kingdom is already here.

A famous instance of the same idea is Jesus' promise to Peter in Matt. 16.18f.: 'And I tell you, you are Peter (Greek *Petros*), and on this rock (Greek *petra*) I will build my church . . . I will give you the keys of the kingdom of heaven, and whatever you bind on earth shall be bound in heaven, and whatever you loose on earth shall be loosed in heaven'. Jesus gives Simon his name-of-destiny, *Rock – Cepha'*, a rock in Aramaic, *Petros* with the male ending *-os* for *petra*, a rock in Greek. Since God has revealed to *him* the secret of Jesus' divinity, God is making him the rock on which the church is to be built. What does this mean? Ever clear, Matthew explains: he is to have *the keys* *of the kingdom of heaven.* This does not mean the popular image of Peter standing by the gates of heaven, letting the nervous Christians in after they die. It means that *whatever he binds or looses on earth,* Christ will ratify *in heaven. Binding* and *loosing* were standard terms in Judaism for saying that something must be done (to keep God's Law), or saying that it need not be done. In ch. 5 we saw Matthew's horror at people like Mark *relaxing* (the same Greek word as *loosing*) *the least commandment.* So Peter will have *the keys of the kingdom of heaven,* that is the supreme authority over the church: what he says, Yes or No, *on earth* will be confirmed by Jesus *in heaven.* So *the kingdom of heaven* is just a way of speaking of *the church.* It is here now, already.

[To have supreme authority over the church is to be, as we would say, *Pope*; but this is not quite what Matthew, let alone Jesus, meant. Paul says that the Pillars 'saw that I had been entrusted with the gospel to the uncircumcision just as Peter had been entrusted with the gospel to the circumcised' (Gal. 2.7): so Peter was generally recognized as the head of the church – Paul says the *Jewish* church. But this has nothing to do with the church at Rome. There is the thinnest evidence that Peter ever went to Rome. He is not referred to in Paul's Roman letter, or in Luke's account of Paul's time at Rome. The association of Peter with Rome is a fiction, a key move in the power struggle to give the Roman church Petrine authority – and a very effective one too. But then the promise to Peter was itself an interpretation of Peter's name designed to give authority to the Petrine movement; we find it only in Matthew's Gospel, in Matthew's style. Luke, a Pauline, took it to mean Peter's heroic leadership in Acts (Luke 22.31–34).]

Matthew thought that the kingdom was here already in the church; but he knew that it was not here in its fullness, and he can take over many of Mark's references to it as in the future. It is he who has Jesus teach the Lord's Prayer, 'Thy kingdom come' (6.10); and he has parables like the Ten Bridesmaids or the Talents, where the kingdom of heaven *will be compared* to the coming of the Bridegroom at midnight, or the return of the master to settle accounts with his servants. But then, of course, Paul's Corinthians knew that the end had not come *completely* yet. We have a prayer in Aramaic, *Maran atha,* 'Our Lord, come!' (I Cor. 16.22). Paul cites it because he wants to stress that the kingdom is still *to come*; and he is able to quote an Aramaic prayer, that is, a prayer from the Jewish church, the Petrine church, and so show that everyone was agreed about things. He was so clever.

At heart Luke was with Paul, his old hero. So he wants to put the coming of the kingdom in the future; and when he reaches the scene where Jesus rides into Jerusalem, and the people shout, 'Blessed is the king who comes in the name of the Lord!' (Luke 19.38), he issues a warning – 'he proceeded to tell a parable, because he was near to Jerusalem, and *because they supposed that the kingdom of God was to appear immediately*' (19.11). The parable is a form of Matthew's Talents, only in Luke's version the rich man is a nobleman who went into a far country to receive a kingdom and then return. The nobleman is a figure for Jesus, who has gone to a *far* country, that is heaven; and it is *there*, not in this world with people shouting Hosanna, that Jesus *receives his kingdom*. The idea that Jesus' kingdom was inaugurated in this life, even on Palm Sunday, was a mistake.

Similarly in Acts 1.6, when Jesus appears to the apostles after the resurrection, Luke makes them ask him, 'Lord, will you at this time restore the *kingdom* to Israel?' Jesus replies, 'It is not for you to know times or seasons . . . But you shall receive power when the Holy Spirit has come upon you'. Luke would hardly have bothered to put this question into the apostles' mouth unless it was a widespread Jerusalem church belief that Jesus had *restored the kingdom to Israel*, at least at the resurrection. Note the surprising phrase, *restore the kingdom to Israel*. Israel had ruled an empire in the days of King David; is Jesus going now to restore this empire, the kingdom of God, with Israel to rule it for him? The answer is No: God alone knows when the kingdom is coming. The big thing now is something different, the coming of the Spirit at Pentecost.

Thus far we have just what we should have expected from a Pauline; but then Luke was such a *friendly* Pauline, and he could never help seeing the Petrine's point of view as well. So he repeats some of the Matthaean sayings in which the kingdom *has* come. At 11.20 he has, 'But if it is by the finger of God that I cast out demons, then the kingdom of God *has come* upon you' – almost word for word the same as Matt. 12.28. Even more striking, he introduces a new

saying with the same force. The Pharisees ask Jesus when the
kingdom of God is coming, and he replies, 'The kingdom of God is
not coming with signs to be observed; nor will they say, Lo, here it
is, or There. For behold, the kingdom of God is in the midst of you'
(17.20f.). The old translation had 'within you', but that must be
wrong, because the kingdom cannot have been within *the Pharisees*!
But there is no mistaking the presence of the kingdom, and the
contrast with its future coming with warning signs. Luke has partly
accepted the Petrine doctrine that the kingdom is present in the
world in the form of the church, even if he supports the Pauline
doctrine a couple of chapters later, at 19.11.

We can sympathize with Luke, for many of the parables contain
the idea of the kingdom being present in the form of seed, which is
going to grow to fullness when the divine harvest comes with Christ's
return; so in a way the kingdom has come, and in another way it is
still ahead. The point seems to the modern reader rather fiddling;
but then the modern reader has not yet seen the effects of the *Already*
doctrine, which so distressed Paul, and which we have to consider in
the next chapters. Some of these effects were the cause of crisis in
the 50s, but they had become less significant forty years later, when
Luke was writing. At the time of I Corinthians they were a hot potato;
but then, as Bernard says in *Yes, Minister*, if you leave a hot potato
alone, in time it will become a cold potato.

7

Tongues and Visions

We have yet to resolve the mystery of why Paul was so sarcastic and angry about the apparently harmless claim that the kingdom was here already; and this becomes clear as it dawns on us what all this meant in practice. The first basis on which the idea rested was the *spiritual gifts* with which the Corinthian church saw itself as being *enriched* (1.5; 4.8). One of these gifts was *words of wisdom* (1.17; 2.1,5,13; 12.8): that is the skill of inferring rules of practical living from passages in the Bible, which I have discussed in chs 4 and 5. But the most exciting, and the most worrying *gifts* were those of tongues, visions and healing, which dominated church meetings at Corinth and elsewhere, and which have made a strong reappearance in the modern church.

Tongues were a new phenomenon, in the sense that we have no evidence of them in the Old Testament, or rabbinic sources. They consisted in individual members of the church being seized by a spirit stronger than themselves, and pouring out a stream of 'words' which were not in their own language. Naturally, some of those who heard caught sounds that sounded like foreign, human languages, and it was sometimes believed that a Greek-speaking Christian was talking Parthian or something. Luke pictures the event of Pentecost like this (Acts 2.1–13), because he says the crowd 'heard [the apostles] speaking each in his own dialect'. Paul kept an open mind on the question: he says, 'Though I speak in the languages of humans and of angels' (I Cor. 13.1). But whether the speech was Parthian or angelic, the miracle was pretty impressive to them. We may be more sceptical. Perhaps the charismatic is deeply stirred by a religious experience, and his attempt to express it is inarticulate; and sometimes, no doubt, there are psychological pressures to join in; and sometimes there may be fraud. I will only say that although I have often heard pulpit anecdotes of charismatics who were heard to be speaking Turkish or Welsh, I have never been able to find reliable evidence that such was the case; and I should be surprised if the Pentecostal movement puts the Language Schools out of business.

Everyone in the early church accepted the validity of 'tongues': Paul says, 'I thank God that I speak in tongues more than you all' (I Cor. 14.18). It was a manifest sign to everyone that if they knew only Greek (and Aramaic, perhaps), and they were talking in Elamite, or, even more marvellous, Angelic, God was at work doing something pretty important. Paul has two anxieties over the business, however: it created chaos, and it was an invitation to manipulation. The church met on Saturday evenings in the home of a well-off member, and started with a meal; but there was no limit on the time and no liturgy. Some members might feel moved to read a passage from scripture, or to give a message ('prophesy'), or to lead some singing; and all these were, as Paul says, *edifying* – they were interesting, and people could join in and feel challenged and stirred. But other members got going in tongues, often three or a dozen at the same time, and there was pandemonium. No one could make himself heard, and visitors might easily think the place a madhouse (14.23). It could go on for hours, and was both boring and frustrating: people might well feel they did not want to come any more.

It has been historically unfortunate that some of the leading charismatics were women. Women were normally not educated in the ancient world, and almost all positions of responsibility were assumed by men; so when an institution appeared in which women were equal, the church, it was inevitable that some of them would compensate by hogging the floor. It is in this context that Paul issues the directive which has given him the name of a misogynist:

Let all things be done for edification. If any speak in a tongue, let there be only two or at the most three, and each in turn; and let one interpret . . . For God is not a God of confusion but of peace. As in all the churches of the saints, the women should keep silence in the churches. For they are not permitted to speak, but should be subordinate, as even the law says (I Cor. 14.27–34).

Actually, by ancient standards, Paul was not a male chauvinist pig. He includes six women by name in his greetings in Rom. 16, and puts Prisca before her husband Aquila; he entrusted the Roman letter to the care of a woman, Phoebe (16.1). But things were out of hand at Corinth, and some of the chief offenders were women; so he imposes order, in a thoroughly defensive and autocratic way. He has the same rule everywhere; this is what the Law says (the *Law*, Paul?); it is shameful for women to speak; if you don't agree with him, you are not recognized (14.34–38). The same unhappy sequence of unreason comes in 11.2–16, where Paul offers the women the choice between wearing their hoods in church or having their hair cut off. Women wore a long robe of heavy material at the time, the *himation*, with a hood which pulled down over the head to the chest, with two eye-holes (and no mouth-hole), like a yashmak. It was not convenient to speak through this to address a public meeting.

The other trouble with tongues (and other claimed spiritual messages) was the scope for manipulating the church. With the tongues-speaker there was often an interpreter, who might say, 'Our sister says she has word from the Spirit . . .'; or people might just 'have a revelation'. Normally this could be quite innocuous, as it is in some independent churches today where time is given to accredited prophets to speak. But what if the 'spirit' should cry out 'Damn Jesus!'? For this is what happened at Corinth:

> I want you to understand that no one speaking by the Spirit of God ever says, Jesus be cursed!; and no one can say, Jesus is Lord!, except by the Holy Spirit (I Cor. 12.3).

It has seemed to many impossible that such a remark could ever have really been made in a church, but for the explanation see ch. 17.

The same peril was latent, and in a more virulent form, in the practice of *visions*, which was also widespread in the early church. Here there was a long tradition, for prophets had had visions of God in the Old Testament: famously Isaiah in Isa. 6, and Ezekiel, whose vision is more detailed, in Ezek. 1. Many Jews had aspired to follow in Ezekiel's steps, and we have their writings over centuries: from the books of Enoch, which go back to perhaps 400 BC, through rabbinic stories about rabbis of the first two centuries AD, and on to the Palaces (*Hekhalot*) literature through the first millennium. The vision of God was the highest aspiration of man. One had to be a saint, or one would die or go mad; one had to keep the Law perfectly, fast for a fortnight, learn Ezek. 1 by heart, put one's head between one's legs, and so on: and then one might be transported to before the divine Throne, and hear the angels.

Paul's anxieties come out in a number of passages. Here is II Cor. 12.1–5:

> I will go on to visions (*optasias*) and revelations (*apokalupseis*) of the Lord. I know a man in Christ who fourteen years ago was caught up to the third heaven – whether in the body or out of the body I do not know, God knows. And I know that this man was caught up to Paradise – whether in the body or out of the body I do not know, God knows – and that he heard things that cannot be told, which man may not utter. On behalf of this man I will boast, but on my own behalf I will not boast, except of my weaknesses.

The passage comes in a series of replies which Paul makes to accusations that he is not a proper apostle: that he is too quiet, is a poor speaker, is over-ambitious, etc. He *goes on to visions and revelations*, because he is accused of not having them. He replies that so far as *visions* are concerned, he knows a (Pauline) Christian who *was caught up to heaven*; for *revelations* he has had so many that God gave him a thorn in the flesh to keep him from pride, but he is not wanting to boast. He makes it clear that the man who had the vision was not himself: *On behalf of this man I will boast, but on my own behalf I will not boast.*

Visions are distinct from *revelations* in that revelations take place on earth, whereas in a vision one is *caught up to heaven*. Paul's friend was caught up to *the third heaven*, or *Paradise*, which is where the Throne of God is. Paul's critics have been discussing whether their experiences were *in the body* or *out of the body*, and Paul is decidedly impatient about such talk – he twice says, *I do not know, God knows*, in a dismissive way. Now of course for Paul's Petrine critics the big thing about such visions was the message they brought back; so Paul says, a little self-righteously, *he heard things that cannot be told, which a man may not utter.* The fact that he makes the point twice like this suggests the contrast: the Petrines have visions and come down and blab divine secrets about them afterwards.

It is the same point about manipulation. There is not much you can say if your fellow-Christian says, 'I have just been taken up to the Throne of God, and there the archangel said to me . . .' You cannot easily reply, 'Well, the archangel is up the creek': he has got you, as they say, over a barrel. We can see this happening at Colosse:

> Therefore let no one pass judgment on you in questions of food and drink or with regard to a festival or a new moon or a sabbath . . . Let no one disqualify you, insisting on self-abasement and worship of angels, taking his stand on visions, puffed up without reason by his sensuous mind . . . (2.16,18).

We have had the first verse before (ch. 5): here are the Petrine evangelists trying to force Pauline converts into observing Jewish ways. But v. 18 shows how the forcing was done. The Petrine would say in the middle of the church meeting, 'Brethren (and sistren), during the prayer-time I was caught up to the Throne, and I beheld God, and the angels praising his glory. And the angel Adiriron (or some impressive name) said to me, I will accompany you to your church. And lo, he is here with me. Down on your faces, all of you, in the presence of the angel!' This is what is implied by the words *taking his stand on visions, insisting on self-abasement and worship of angels.* Of course the angel then told the hapless Colossians that they should not be eating non-*kosher* meat or working on sabbath and so on; and if the Pauline tried to object, they *disqualified* him – 'Well, if you will not even do what the angel says, you're not a proper Christian, and had better leave'. It is a marvellous move: it is surprising that it is not done more widely.

The Paulines could see that this had got to be stopped, so they fell back on a second tradition in the Old Testament. Sometimes Isaiah or Ezekiel or Daniel may be portrayed as seeing God; but at other times Moses, for example, is told that he may *not* see God's face – 'you cannot see my face; for man shall not see me and live' (Ex. 33.20). So we find in John:

For the law was given through Moses; grace and truth came through Jesus Christ. No one has ever seen God; the only Son, who is in the bosom of the Father, he has made him known (John 1.17f.).

John makes it clear that the visionaries are *Petrines*: they are Jewish Christians who are keen on *the Law*. He says the Law was only the first step, through *Moses*, a man; the fullness of *grace and truth*, mentioned in Ex. 34, came *through Jesus Christ, God's Son*, who has really *made him known*. Claims of visions are overridden by the incarnation which has let us see God as he really is, in Jesus; just as claims about the Law are overridden by Jesus. In fact *no one has ever seen God*, as it says in Ex. 33.

Similarly at John 3.13, Jesus says to Nicodemus, 'No one has ascended into heaven but he who descended from heaven, the Son of Man, who is in heaven'. This is the second time we have heard John saying *No one has* . . . This kind of denial is sometimes called a *table-thumping negative*: people who deny something with emphasis more than once usually do so because someone is saying the opposite. So here, Nicodemus is (ch. 6) a pattern Jewish Christian, a half-believing Petrine, as John thinks of him: so John has Jesus tell him that anyone who talks about his having *ascended into heaven* is a liar. Only Jesus has done that, after he had first *descended from heaven*, and that is where he is now, *in heaven*. Or again, at 6.46 Jesus says to *the Jews*, 'Not that anyone has seen the Father, except him who is from God; he has seen the Father' (6.46). Or Jesus says to Philip, 'He who has seen me has seen the Father' (14.6). Perhaps some of Philip's converts may have been keen on visions; John is telling them that it is not necessary now Jesus has come.

In view of this it is the more striking that we have an actual description of God as seen in a vision on the Throne in the New Testament: it comes in Rev. 4, where John the Seer (a different John) is summoned up to heaven in the Spirit,

and lo, a throne stood in heaven, with one seated on the throne! And he who sat there appeared like jasper and carnelian, and round the throne was a rainbow that looked like an emerald . . . (Rev. 4.3).

The description of the Throne, and of God himself, and of the living creatures, is a combination of details from Ezek. 1, Isa. 6, Ex. 19 and some Christian additions; so even the Paulines who selected the books which make up the New Testament did not draw the line at *a Pauline* seeing God. For the Seer is a Pauline, though he is very sympathetic to the Jewish mission too, as we shall see. Also the vision does not end with an angel telling the church to keep sabbath; but rather gives a prophecy of things to come, which was much more to the taste of the Paulines.

An interesting light on the visions comes in I Timothy, a letter written by a rather uncharitable Pauline known as the Pastor, in Paul's name, but forty years after his death. He speaks of 'the blessed and only Sovereign, the King of kings and Lord of lords, who alone has immortality and dwells in unapproachable light, whom no man has ever seen or can see' (6.15f.); and soon after says, 'Avoid the godless chatter and contradictions of what is falsely called knowledge' (Greek *gnosis*, 6.20). The Pastor is keen on the table-thumping negative, like John the evangelist: *unapproachable* light, *whom no man has ever seen or can see.* The opposition (who are Petrines, 'desiring to be teachers of *the Law*, without understanding what they are saying . . .', 1.7) are claiming to have seen God, and are twice told emphatically that this is impossible. They are also twice told that God is the *only* Sovereign, and that he *alone* has immortality: so we are up against a development in which there is more than one 'power' in heaven. The Jewish Christians who make these assertions claim to have *knowledge* that they are so; and it looks as if this *knowledge* is thought to be given in heavenly visions. In time there grew to be a formidable wing of the church which taught that there was more than one power in heaven, and they were known as *Gnostics*, Christians who think that they have *knowledge* or *gnosis*.

The vision thing, as Mr Bush would say, was not new in II Corinthians. Petrines talked about *words of knowledge* in I Cor. 12.8: that is rulings delivered by angels seen in visions, just as *words of wisdom* were rulings delivered by arguments from scripture. Paul says that if the Jewish rulers had *known*, they would not have had Jesus crucified; he was the Lord of Glory, something that *no eye has seen* (I Cor. 2.8f.; Isa. 64.4). *Knowledge*, he says later, is imperfect and temporary: 'For now we see through a mirror dimly, but then face to face. Now I *know* in part; then I shall *know* fully, even as I have been fully *known*' (I Cor. 13.12). But seeing God and the *knowledge* supposed to come from it, do not hold a candle to *love*.

8

The Gifts and the Fruits of the Spirit

Paul deals with the problem of tongues, visions, healings, etc. in three chapters of I Corinthians, I Cor. 12–14, which include the most famous piece he ever wrote, I Cor. 13, the passage on love which is often used at weddings. His handling of the problem is masterly, and should be a compulsory study in courses on management. We can all learn from it.

The real issue, as becomes clear in ch. 14, is how the precious time of church worship is to be used, and the only two options discussed are tongues and 'prophecy' (inspiring short sermons, we might say). Paul wants tongues to be kept as short as possible, and the edifying prophecies to be given free rein. But he has more sense than to say so at once (to be 'confrontational'). He uses his wits. First he sets out a list of *nine* different gifts of the Spirit, on the honoured principle, Divide and muddle: if there are nine gifts, then we are not choosing between two of them. Then comes a long spiel of sweet reasonableness: we are all one body, brethren, and the eye needs the hand, and the foot needs the nose. Paul knows how to be obvious and boring, and this can be very helpful at meetings. Then he puts the gifts in order, numbering them with his own preferred ones top and the ones he is not so keen on last; concentration has lapsed a bit, and it is easy not to notice this key move. Then he lifts the level of the whole discussion: 'And I will show you a still more excellent way' – the way of love (ch. 13). Then, when he has come to the real issue, in ch. 14, he has won the battle before fighting it. This is what my old Theological College principal used to call Holy Guile.

It is instructive to put the two lists of gifts alongside each other, the one from 12.8–10, perhaps as the Petrines saw them, and the other from 12.28, as Paul saw them:

Words of Wisdom	Apostles
Words of Knowledge	Prophets
Faith	Teachers
Gifts of Healing	Workers of Miracles
Working of Miracles	Healers
Prophecy	Helpers
Distinguishing Spirits	Administrators
Various Tongues	Speakers in Various Tongues
Interpretation of Tongues	[Interpreters, v.29]

We may notice three things.

1. Some gifts in the first list have disappeared in the second: especially the first two. Now Paul spent a lot of energy in chs 1–2 explaining that *words of wisdom* were nothing to the gospel of the cross (they were *taught words of human wisdom* as opposed to God's wisdom, the mystery of Jesus' crucifixion). In the last chapter we saw how dangerous visions were, with the *words of knowledge* which they produced. So Paul quietly forgets about these. 'Distinguishing spirits' also drops out, but that is more accidental: Paul wants people to distinguish the Holy Spirit's utterances from those of demons (12.1–3).

2. He has quietly *inserted* a number of new gifts – apostleship, teaching, 'helping', administering. These have in common a certain workaday quality; they are not exciting; in fact it will have come as a surprise to the Petrines that they should have been called gifts at all. But if it is a gift to be a prophet, it is difficult to deny the status to the higher calling of being an apostle. Of course there is only one apostle around, and that is Paul; and the Paulines, who made less of a splash with the tongues and visions side of things, were given dignity if their humble help were recognized in contributing money, or organizing its distribution.

3. He has *changed the order* significantly. This is done partly by putting his own gift, apostleship, first, and by promoting the gift he values, prophecy, to the second place, while leaving tongues and their interpretation at the bottom of the list. Teaching, an 'ordinary' gift, and one important to Paulines, is similarly placed third, ahead of miracles. But the ordering is also emphasized by the introduction of numbers – *first apostles, second prophets, third teachers*; and then by

concluding, 'But earnestly desire the *higher* gifts' (12.31). The
Petrine charismatic, so proud of his (or her) visions, tongues or
revelations, is left feeling rather low down the batting order. It seems
as if the gifts that matter are mostly in the hands of Paulines.

Paul's treatment of the problem over gifts is thus masterly; but
something still remains to be said about the controversial question
of healings. It is probable that the three separate items in the left-
hand column, *faith, healing, working of miracles*, refer in different ways
to the same phenomena, the healing of sick people by confident
words (prayers, exorcisms, etc.) with or without sacramental symbols
(oil, spittle, laying on of hands). Paul does say, 'If I have all faith so
as to remove mountains' (13.2); and we may have to think of words
of cursing, causing blindness (Acts 13.11) or death (Acts 5.1–11); or
of the multiplication of food: but the most likely thing, or at least the
most normal, is healing.

Healing remains a controversial matter, because there is no lack
of 'spiritual healers' today, and strong assertions of the validity of
such methods are to be heard alongside strong denials. It might be
agreed that: (*a*) only a proportion of those who are prayed over
recover: on one count, of those attending healing services in Britain,
9% claimed to have been wholly or partly healed. (*b*) It is wrong to
blame failure to be healed on lack of faith. Some quite casual
attenders are made better while some very earnest believers are not;
the 'lack of faith' charge is an easy escape for the healer, and a cause
of deep depression to the unhealed. (*c*) People's bodies are not
machines which respond only to drugs and surgery; they are a
psycho-somatic (body-and-soul) unity, and may well respond to
positive mental influences. The study of such interactions has a long
way to go, but there is discussion of certain (T4) cells which may be
the means of such influence. (*d*) When people are taken out of a
lonely, poverty-stricken, hopeless environment, and surrounded by
cheerful, kindly people who provide for them and look after them, as
for example on trains going to Lourdes, it is not surprising if they *feel*
better; and an important part of 'being healed' is feeling better.
(*e*) The more a community accepts the possibility of spiritual healing,
the more it will try it, and the more claims of healing there are likely
to be.

Now for one reason or another, healings were a feature of the

Jerusalem mission in a way that they were not of the Pauline mission; and naturally the Petrines drew attention to this. The accusations about Paul's failure to have visions (II Cor. 12.1–10) are followed by the defensive comment:

> The signs of a true apostle were performed among you in all endurance, in signs and wonders and mighty works (12.12).

We can tell that this is a response to the Petrines because Paul says just before: 'Are they Hebrews? So am I. Are they Israelites? So am I . . .' (11.22). They were *Jewish Christians*, proud of being Israelites and the seed of Abraham, and contemptuous of Paul and his Gentile converts – he was no great miracle-worker. Oh, yes I am, replies the apostle; the real *signs of an apostle* were indeed performed among you in Corinth. They were not the occasional sick person made better; they were *in all endurance*. Now Paul has used the same word *endurance* before of the numerous afflictions which he has been through as an apostle: 'as servants of God we commend ourselves in every way: through *great endurance*, in afflictions, hardships, calamities . . .' (II Cor. 6.4f.). The signs of a true apostle were his sufferings for the faith. Perhaps it was at Corinth that Paul received one of his five thrashings in the synagogue (II Cor. 11.24), or one of the three formidable canings he had from the Roman authorities (11.25). His occasions of enduring these were signs, wonders and mighty works, more impressive to the eye of faith than many exorcisms.

We meet other echoes of the same problem. In I Cor. 1 Paul is contrasting his majestic gospel of the cross with the Petrines' claims to *words of wisdom*; and he adds, 'For Jews demand signs and Greeks seek wisdom, but we preach Christ crucified' (1.22). Paul is not complaining about the difficulty of converting non-Christian Jews and Greeks: the problems are inside the church. Greek (Gentile) church-members are over-impressed with Petrine talk about *wisdom*, what Paul calls *taught words of human wisdom*; and Jewish Christians are over-impressed by *signs*, by some striking apparent response to prayer. What Paul has to offer is something more marvellous than either of these, God's mysterious wisdom shown in the cross.

It has often been noticed similarly, that in Luke's account in Acts,

Paul seems to be keeping pace with Peter in the miracles he does. Peter and John heal a lame man in the Temple (Acts 3), and Paul a lame man at Lystra (Acts 14). Peter heals the paralysed Aeneas, and raises the dead Dorcas to life (Acts 9); Paul raises the dead Eutychus to life (Acts 20), and restores the sick Publius in Acts 28. But somehow Paul's miracles fail quite to impress as Peter's do. Publius had nothing worse than a fever and dysentery (28.8); and we wonder if Eutychus was quite dead, because Paul falls upon him and says, 'Do not be alarmed, for his life is in him' (20.10). So it seems as if Luke is doing his best to keep the scores level; for Paul to keep up with the Jerusalem Jones's.

Paul believed in the gifts of the Spirit (in a way that many modern churchmen do not), but he knew that in this field the Petrines had the legs of him. However Paul was a profoundly religious man, and even if he knows how to play management games, this is not what Christianity was about. The most impressive effects of the Holy Spirit to him, as to many today, are in its apparent power to transform human life, in its ability to inspire virtue, and the heroic virtue we call holiness. Hence an important distinction which Paul introduces, between the *gifts* and the *fruit* of the Spirit. *Gifts* are something which you may or may not have been given, very nice to have, and a responsibility to use for the good of the community; but *fruit* is something which comes naturally and inevitably from being part of an organism, and may be expected of everyone. The image is quite widely used: Matthew says that every tree which does not bear good fruit is cut down and thrown into the fire (3.10).

In Paul's discussion of gifts in I Corinthians, he closes his numbered list in ch. 12,

> But earnestly desire the higher gifts. And I will show you a still more excellent way. If I speak in the tongues of men and of angels, but have not love, I am a noisy gong or a clanging cymbal. And if I have prophetic powers, and understand all mysteries and all knowledge, and if I have all faith, so as to remove mountains, but have not love, I am nothing. If I give away all that I have, and if I devote my body so as to boast, but have not love, I gain nothing.

Paul has set out the *gifts*, and he wants his converts to aspire to *the higher gifts* – apostleship, prophecy, teaching. But he turns to show *a still more excellent way*, that of *love*, which is not a gift, but something everyone must have, and without which all the gifts are *nothing*. *Tongues*, identified as either human or angelic, *prophecy, knowledge* of divine *mysteries* delivered in visions, *faith* to work healings and miracles, *giving* of one's possessions to the church (see ch. 10), asceticism in the *devotion of one's body* (see ch.9): all of these gifts offer *no profit* unless there is *love*. The familiar translation has 'though I give my body to be burned', but 'burned' (*kauthesomai*) is only one letter different from 'boast' (*kauchesomai*), which stands in the oldest tradition and gives better sense. Tongues, knowledge, even Paul's favoured prophecy, are *imperfect* and *will pass away*. The only things that will *abide*, on into the age to come, are *faith* (in God and in Christ, not miracle-working), *hope and love; but the greatest of these is love*.

We have seen the cardinal place which Paul gives to love, as the *fulfilment of the Law* (ch.5). One place where Paul says this is Gal. 5.14, and he continues:

> But I say, walk by the Spirit, and do not gratify the desires of the flesh . . . Now the works of the flesh are plain: fornication, impurity, licentiousness, idolatry, sorcery, enmity, strife, jealousy, anger, selfishness, dissension, party spirit, envy, drunkenness, carousing and the like. I warn you, as I warned you before, that those who do such things shall not inherit the kingdom of God. But the fruit of the Spirit is love, joy, peace, patience, kindness, goodness, faithfulness, gentleness, self-control; against such there is no Law (5.16–23).

Once more we are in the hands of the master. Oh yes, agrees the Petrine reader, as he hears *the works of the flesh* listed. These are what I never do – fornication, idolatry, sorcery, they are all condemned in the Torah. But then comes a whole sequence of things not condemned in the Torah, but which are the wreck of Christian charity in the Galatian churches (5.15, 25f.): enmity, strife and so on – Paul has quite an extensive vocabulary. But *the fruit of the Spirit is love, joy, peace* . . . There is no provision in *the Law* against these. If we have the Spirit, *let us walk in it*. It is the means to a transformed, Christian life.

To the Petrine movement Paul was a twister (*panourgos*, II Cor. 12.16). The Christian faith rested on three foundations: Jesus' proclamation of the present arrival of the kingdom, evidenced in healings and other marvellous events; the resurrection, to which Peter and James and the others had been the prime witnesses; and the abundant evidence of the Spirit of God – in the gift of foreign (and even heavenly) languages, in visions where saints were caught up to heaven and were given revelations by the angels, in miraculous healings and other infallible proofs. Paul denied the presence of the kingdom; he had a lop-sided doctrine of the resurrection (ch. 23); and neither he nor his followers could make much of a showing with tongues, visions or miracles. Talk about teachers and administrators having *gifts* was a get-out, and sermons about love, joy and peace missed the point. These things were not impressive; they had all been around before Jesus was heard of.

To Paul, Petrine religion was all froth and show. It was marvellous that the Spirit had come, and his presence was irrefutable evidence of the truth of the gospel. He did indeed inspire mysterious language, and revelations a-plenty to Paulines and Petrines alike. Every Christian knew something of the ecstasy of prayer, as 'the Spirit intercedes for us with sighs too deep for words' (Rom. 8.26). But the Spirit was not confined to the glasshouse atmosphere of the church-meeting (where He must be scandalized by the indiscipline and chaos). He was to be seen in the crisis of missionary life, when often Christ's representative was pulled off to be scourged, or when he shivered and starved for lack of a charitable home for the night. That was where the *signs* of the spirit were to be seen. Or as the simple Christian went about his way in kindness and forgiveness and gentleness of heart: there was the transforming Spirit in action. I am a great admirer of the saint myself. This is a religion worth something; a great treasure which the secularizing world will lose at its peril.

9

Radicalism I: Sex

One of the things which Petrines did was to 'hand over their bodies' – 'if I hand over my body so as to boast', says Paul, a little uncharitably (I Cor. 13.3). This presumably means that they *devoted* their bodies *to God*, or in other words took the kind of vows we associate with the monastic life, and that you heard a lot about it afterwards. Why should people do that? Well, in the first place they felt that now that the kingdom had come they were on a different, *spiritual* level; and that they were now above all *fleshly* desires, the most obvious of which was sex.

> The natural (*psychikos*) man does not receive the gifts of the Spirit of God, for they are folly to him. The spiritual (*pneumatikos*) man judges all things, but is himself judged by no one ... But I, brethren, could not address you as spiritual men, but as fleshly, as babes in Christ ... For while there is jealousy and strife among you, are you not fleshly? (I Cor. 2.14–3.3).

The Petrines drew the distinction on the basis of the book of Genesis. There the creation of man is described twice. At Gen. 1.27 'God created man in his own image', and at Gen. 2.7 God 'breathed into his nostrils the breath of life, and man became a living soul (*psyche*)'. We should say that the two accounts stem from two different authors, but the Jews, as we learn from Philo, a contemporary of Paul, often saw them as two different creations. The Genesis 1 Man was a being in the spiritual world, looking exactly like God (*in his Image*), while the Genesis 2 man was moulded out of clay and only rose to the level of a soul (*psyche*). So ordinary mortals were *natural, fleshly* people; but the baptized Jewish-Christian had moved on to the *spiritual* plane, in line with the Gen. 1 Man. Paul laughs at his presumption in a kindly way. All the talk about being spiritual does not fit very well with the quarrels and jealousies reported to him: it all sounds pretty *fleshly* still! There is some more about the *natural* and the *spiritual* Men in I Cor. 15.44–49.

The *spiritual* Petrines also claimed to be *perfect*: Paul says, 'Yet among the perfect we do impart wisdom' (2.6) – he accepts them at their own face value, as spiritual and perfect Christians. But actually Paul was horrified at such grandiloquence. He says later,

> Not that I have already obtained [the resurrection] or am already perfected; but I press on to make it my own, because Christ Jesus has made me his own. Brethren, I do not consider that I have made it my own; . . . but I press on towards the goal for the prize of the upward call of God in Christ Jesus. Let those of us who are perfect be thus minded (Phil. 3.12ff.).

Petrines may claim to have a share in the resurrected life already, and to be perfect; not so Paul, who is pressing on towards the goal, longing to attain it. He still plays along with the word, *those of us who are perfect*, but he takes away the meaning.

If you were spiritual and perfect, then you were above the desires of the flesh, and this then suggested that married couples should give up sexual relations. Paul's converts at Corinth wrote to ask his opinion about this:

> Now concerning the things about which you wrote. It is well for a man not to touch a woman. But because of the temptation to immorality, each man should have his own wife and each woman her own husband. The husband should give to his wife her conjugal rights, and likewise the wife to her husband . . . Do not refuse one another except perhaps by agreement for a season, that you may devote yourselves to prayer; but then come together again, lest Satan tempt you through lack of self-control (I Cor. 7.1–5).

Abstinence is fine, says Paul; but he knows about the power of the sex drive, and the folly of denying it. So he counsels normal marital relations. If they like, they can give it up for Lent, so to speak; but aiming too high can be unrealistic and lead to disaster. Paul goes on to say that he is quite fulfilled as a celibate, and wishes everyone was like him; but then he knows they are not. We may note that the point of giving sex up is said to be 'that you may devote yourselves to prayer'. It is quite likely that the prayer was associated with aspirations to vision, that one might see the Divine Throne; for it was often thought that abstinence from food, sex and other normal appetites was a preparation for such an experience.

The Corinthians asked similarly about not getting married, or remarried:

> To the unmarried and the widows I say that it is well for them to remain single as I do. But if they cannot exercise self-control, they should marry. For it is better to marry than to be aflame with passion. If anyone thinks that he is not behaving properly towards his girl-friend, if his passions are strong, and it has to be, let him do as he wishes: let them marry – it is no sin. But whoever is firmly established in his heart, being under no necessity . . . to keep her as his girl-friend, he will do well (7.8f., 36f.).

Paul would prefer everyone not married to remain celibate, for two reasons. He thought the end of the world was only a few years away, and that this, in line with Old Testament prophecy, would be preceded by a time of appalling suffering ('the impending distress', 7.26, 'the appointed time has grown very short', 7.29, 'I would spare you tribulation', 7.28); it would be bad enough for adults fleeing to the mountains, but dreadful for those pregnant, or carrying young children. Then also, married couples have to give a lot of energy to looking after one another, whereas the celibate can give their whole lives to serving Christ (7.32–35). Nevertheless, realism means that in most cases, if young couples are in love they had better marry.

This leads on to a third question, and to a couple of sentences in which Paul has been very widely misunderstood:

> To the married I give charge, not I but the Lord, that the wife should not separate from her husband (but if she does, let her

remain single, or else be reconciled to her husband) – and that the husband should not divorce his wife (7.10f.).

Today people cannot think of any other reason for getting divorced except 'incompatibility', or desire for a new partner; but the context shows a very un-modern motive to be much more likely. The Corinthians have asked whether married couples should abstain from sex, and unmarried people abstain from marriage; so the natural suggestion is that married couples should separate for the same reason. After all, if you are determined to live on the high spiritual plane, you do make it difficult for yourself if you go to bed each night with an attractive young woman whom you are fond of. Furthermore, if the husband is off on mission for the church, the question is bound to arise whether the wife should not be free to marry elsewhere, and so be provided for. Notice that it is the *wife's separating* which is mentioned first; and that she is forbidden to remarry, which is not envisaged at all for her husband. If she *does* separate, she must keep herself, or else go back to her man.

A further significant point is that this matter, and this only, is said to be authorized by Jesus himself – 'I give charge, not I *but the Lord*'. This situation must have arisen in Jesus' ministry. We may imagine the scene in Peter's kitchen. 'The most amazing news, dear. The prophet Jesus has called me to be one of his first disciples. We're going off on mission tomorrow.' 'That's nice, dear: who's going to run the boat and pay for the kids?' Jesus chose married men, like Peter, with mothers-in-law, to be among his followers and to be away from home for weeks and months. There must have been cases where the financial and emotional strain was too much, and it was asked, 'Should we divorce?' Jesus replied, 'Certainly not: God made marriage to be for life' (Mark 10.7ff.). The rules laid down by Jesus in Mark 10.2–12 are identical with those which Paul cites in I Cor. 7. Mark gives them in the context of 'Pharisees, tempting him'; but then Mark thought of James and the rest of Jesus' family in Jerusalem as Pharisees. Eight times in his Gospel we find Pharisees disputing with Jesus, and always about issues which the Jerusalem leaders disputed with the Paulines. Eight times Jesus agrees with Paul.

Matthew retells the story of the Pharisees asking about divorce; but by Matthew's time the high aspirations of the first generation were in retreat, and more modern motives for divorce were in evidence. The Law said that a man should divorce his wife if he found in her 'the unseemly thing' (Deut. 24.1), and the Sages discussed whether this meant adultery (Shammai), or burning the dinner (Hillel). So in Matthew the Pharisees ask, 'Is it lawful to divorce one's wife *for any reason* [as the Hillelites say]?'; and Jesus replies that divorce and remarriage are wrong *except in cases of unchastity* (Matt. 19.9). In other words, Jesus takes the Shammaites' line.

At the close of the incident the disciples comment, 'If such is the case of a man with his wife, it is not expedient to marry' (19.10). They do not mean, 'If you cannot get divorced easily, it is better to live in sin': the thought is how to combine being a disciple with the duties of marriage. Jesus replies that some men are eunuchs from birth and others are castrated; 'and there are eunuchs who have made themselves eunuchs for the sake of the kingdom of heaven. He who is able to receive this, let him receive it' (19.12). Matthew allows space for the higher holiness of the Petrines. They can give up sex for life if they feel called to it. At the same time he is closer to Paul in resisting any attempt to impose such standards on all Christians. This is only for *him who is able to receive it – not for all men, but only those to whom it is given* (19.11); Paul says that he had the gift of celibate continence and wished others did too, but he recognized that this was not so. Most modern interpreters understand 'have made themselves eunuchs for the sake of the kingdom' as *metaphorical*; but many ancient interpreters thought it was intended literally, and the great scholar Origen took it so, and acted on it.

We find a series of echoes of this controversy in Pauline writings later. In John 2 Jesus attends a wedding at Cana, and provides a large volume of wine at it: this gives the impression, and is probably intended to give the impression, that Jesus thought marriage was a good thing, and drinking wine within (rather wide) limits was all right too. Hebrews says, 'Let marriage be held in honour among all' (13.4) I Tim 4.1–3 is clear:

Now the Spirit expressly says that in later times some will depart from the faith by giving heed to deceitful spirits and doctrines of demons, through the pretensions of liars whose consciences are seared, who forbid marriage and enjoin abstinence from foods which God created to be received with thanksgiving by those who believe and know the truth.

The Pastor, in his moderate and kindly way, is countering the teachings of the Petrines (*liars whose consciences are seared*), and whom he unchurches as heretics (*will depart from the faith*). They claim to receive inspiration from angels (*giving heed to deceitful spirits and doctrines of demons*). The particular doctrines which are so dangerous are that they *forbid marriage, and enjoin abstinence from foods*. They are in fact Jewish Christians, Petrines who are aiming for a higher holiness, with abstinence from marriage, and with food-laws. Indeed their Jewish sympathies come in a number of other texts (I Tim. 1.6f.; Titus 1.10,14); but this is the clearest indication that the ascetic enthusiasm countered by Paul in I Cor. 7 is still strong half a century later.

Revelation is a book written by a seer with sympathies for both the missions. In Rev. 7 there are two great wings of the church. There are 144,000 sealed 'out of every tribe of the sons of Israel'; the twelve tribes are named, and there are 12,000 sealed from each tribe. But then, 'After this I looked, and behold, a great multitude which no man could number, from every nation, from all tribes and peoples and tongues, standing before the Lamb' (7.9). In other words there is a Jewish Christian church and a Gentile church – and the latter is beginning to outnumber the former. This pattern is repeated in Rev. 14:

Then I looked, and lo, on Mount Zion stood the Lamb, and with him a hundred and forty-four thousand who had his name and his Father's name written on their foreheads . . . It is these who have not defiled themselves with women, for they are virgins; it is these who follow the Lamb wherever he goes . . . Then I saw another angel flying in mid-heaven, with an eternal gospel to proclaim to those who dwell on earth, to every nation and tribe and tongue and people (Rev. 14.1,4,6).

The 144,000, as in Rev. 7, are the Jewish Christians, and that is why they are *on Mount Zion*, the mountain on which Jerusalem stands, the home of the Jewish Christian church. They have Christ's name on their foreheads, for they are Christians; but also *his Father's name*, Yahweh, because they are *Jewish* Christians. Jewish Christianity had put away sex as being fleshly, and in consequence its members were *virgins*, and *had not* (in their own view, with which the Seer sympathizes) *defiled themselves with women*. (I am afraid that his thinking is rather male-oriented, as they say; there is no mention of any virgin women being redeemed, who have not defiled themselves with men.) But the Jewish church is only the first element of redemption (compare Rom. 1.16, 'to the Jew first and also to the Greek'). There follows *another angel* proclaiming the gospel to *every nation and tribe and tongue and people*, as in 7.9; and in 14.14ff. the sickle is put in, and the harvest of the earth, that is the Gentile church, is gathered in. So the Seer is very conscious of the two missions as being distinct, and each bound for heaven; and the feature which he especially identifies as special to the Jewish mission is its abstention from sexual relations, and so virginity.

Abstention from sex was to have a long future. Eusebius tells us of a movement in central Turkey in the second century, with its centre in a small town called Pepuza. The leader was a man called Montanus at first, but he was succeeded by two powerful women, Maximilla and Priscilla. The movement laid stress on ecstasies, revelations, visions and heavenly ascents, just like the first-century Petrines; and Maximilla and Priscilla divorced their husbands, as the Corinthian Petrines wished to, probably with a view to having visions (*Ecclesiastical History*, 5.16–19). Their most famous convert was the African Father Tertullian, a formidable man who much emphasized the importance of virginity; and the indirect influence of Jewish Christianity has been felt ever since through the anti-sexual writings of Augustine. The Jewish Christians had a more direct influence on the Syrian church, which they had founded; where for centuries baptism was understood to involve a vow of celibacy. So those who are critical of St Paul for his attitude to sex should think again; his is the voice of liberalism and commonsense, for which he deserves much credit. But we should not be blind to the nobility of Petrine aspirations; they *handed over their bodies* to God, and many of their successors have found fulfilment in monasteries and mission fields. Perhaps their reward will be great in heaven, besides.

10

Radicalism II: Money

I mentioned the problem of paying for Mrs Peter's keep; but there was the equally serious question of feeding the considerable group of Jesus' full-time disciples. Luke tells us how it was resolved:

> Soon afterward he went through towns and villages, preaching and bringing the good news of the kingdom of God. And the twelve were with him, and also some women who had been healed . . . Mary called Magdalene . . . and Joanna the wife of Chuza, Herod's steward, and Susanna, and many others, who provided for them out of their means (Luke 8.1ff.).

The party consists of thirteen men and three named women and 'many' others; Luke sometimes uses 'many' in a rather exaggerated way, but we may think of the group as approaching twenty. Anyone who has fed twenty people for a week in modern times will know that the expense is not negligible, and the Gospels give us the impression that Jesus' ministry went on for months, perhaps a couple of years. Perhaps Joanna was available because she was a widow; and perhaps, as Herod's treasurer, Chuza had been quite well paid. At all events it was the accepted practice for the movement to share a common purse. Judas kept this purse, according to John, and stole from it (John 12.6).

After Jesus' death this pattern of sharing money continued:

> And all who believed were together and had all things in common; and they sold their possessions and goods, and distributed them to all, as any had need. And day by day, attending the temple

together and breaking bread in their homes, they shared food with rejoicing and generosity of heart (Acts 2.44ff.).

Later Luke tells how Barnabas sold a farm of his in Cyprus and donated the money to the church; and how, less happily, a couple called Ananias and Sapphira sold a property and pretended to give all the money to the apostles, but kept part of it back. They were struck dead for lying to the Holy Spirit.

Scholars have sometimes accused Luke of romanticizing the primitive church, generalizing from the actions of Barnabas and one or two others. But with such scepticism we cannot understand the first Christians, and the dynamic movement of which they were part. The kingdom had arrived; the end of the world was here; money would be of no value when the Lord came. What mattered was that we had been called into the kingdom. Those who could should devote their whole energies to spreading the word, to prayer, to healing meetings, to pastoral visiting, etc.; and those who had resources should contribute them to the common pool to enable this to go on. Luke draws an attractive picture of the church supper. The money has been given in 'generosity of heart', and the poorer Christians, who may often have been hungry, 'shared food' in plenty; and there was 'rejoicing', *agalliasis*, the rare joy that comes to people who share unreservedly in a great common enterprise.

Radicalism of this kind draws our admiration; but it also draws a certain nervous caution. How long will the money from Barnabas' farm last? The number of converts seems to have been rather large (Acts 2.41), and there seem to have been quite a lot of widows to be provided for (6.1); experience suggests that regular free meals may have been an encouragement to conversions. In any case we have signs that the Jerusalem church was under financial strain fifteen years later, for when Paul visited the Pillars in 48, 'they would have us remember the poor, which very thing I was eager to do' (Gal. 2.10). They were not worried about the poor of Ethiopia, but about the poor of the Jerusalem church, whom they did not have sufficient money to feed properly. If Paul was converting all these rich Gentiles, perhaps he could raise a collection? Paul was indeed eager to respond; he knew that if he could raise a good sum, the Jerusalem church would be less scrupulous about the doctrines he taught in his mission.

In time the Jerusalem church fell on evil days. They had to leave the city when the Jewish War came (66), and were not allowed to return after it was destroyed in 70. They were scattered to various centres in Syria, and became known as the *'Ebionim*, the Poor, a term often used in the Psalms for God's faithful, persecuted remnant. Epiphanius, Bishop of Salamis in Cyprus about 370, questioned some of them and asked them about their name; they replied that they were descended from the Jerusalem church, and their forebears had become poor by sharing their money in the days of the Acts. Epiphanius, a harsh and untruthful man himself, thought that they were lying: they were called Ebionites after their wicked first teacher Ebion (*Panarion*, 30.15.4). But we may think they were telling the truth: there never was such a person as Ebion.

When Paul went on his mission to Greece, he had as his companion Silas, a respected Jerusalem Christian (Acts 15.27,32,40). This meant that his message had Jerusalem authority, but it also meant muddle and tension, because Silas encouraged practices which Paul was not keen on, like giving up work and sharing money:

> But concerning love of the brethren you have no need to have anyone write to you . . . But we exhort you, brethren, to do so more and more, to aspire to live quietly, to mind your own affairs, and to work with your hands, as we charged you; so that you may command the respect of outsiders, and be dependent on nobody (I Thess. 4.9–12).

The Christians at Thessalonica (Saloniki in modern Greece) have accepted the gospel with marvellous enthusiasm, and have been sharing their money with fellow-Christians (*love of the brethren*), not only in their own church but in other churches in Macedonia (northern Greece). Splendid!, says Paul; but do keep working (*mind your own affairs, work with your hands*), or you will be despised by non-believers, and you will become paupers. According to Luke Paul was only three weeks in the town (Acts 17.1–9), but the habit of stopping work had already started while he was there (*as we charged you*), and it must have been due to Silas' Jerusalem influence.

Paul went on to start the church at Corinth on his own, while Silas stayed behind in Macedonia (Acts 17.14; 18.5; I Thess. 3.1); so it is not surprising that the enthusiasm continued. Paul wrote a second letter, taking up the point at length:

> Now we command you, brethren, in the name of our Lord Jesus Christ, that you keep away from any brother who is living in idleness and not in accord with the tradition which you received from us. For you yourselves know how you ought to imitate us; we were not idle when we were with you, we did not eat anyone's bread without paying, but with toil and labour we worked night and day, that we might not burden any of you. It was not because we have not that right, but to give you in our conduct an example to imitate. For even when we were with you, we gave you this command: if anyone will not work, neither let him eat. For we hear that some of you are living in idleness, mere busybodies, not doing any work. Now such persons we command and exhort in the name of the Lord Jesus Christ to do their work in quietness and to earn their own living (II Thess. 3.6–12).

Things have got out of hand, and Paul applies the discipline of shunning, indeed excommunication: the church is to *keep away from any who is living in idleness, not doing any work.* 'Note that man, and have nothing to do with him, that he may be ashamed', he adds (3.14). Paul himself had worked while he was among them, and *given an example to imitate.* Work was *the tradition which you received from us, we gave you this command.* It is from this context that Mrs Thatcher drew her famous text, *If anyone will not work, neither let him eat.* There is not the least suggestion that they are lazy; on the contrary, they are *busybodying* – or, from a less prejudiced angle, going round on pastoral visits, praying with the sick, organizing missionary meetings, distributing charity, and generally doing the Lord's work. Silas must have been proud of them.

Paul was not very pleased with Silas, and it is no surprise that he disappears from the story in Acts soon after he joins Paul at Corinth, as he does from the headings of Paul's letters. But the same problem recurs there, in a passage we have already noticed (ch. 4):

> Already you are stuffed! Already you have become rich! Without us you have begun to reign! And would that you did reign, so that

we might share the reign with you! . . . To the present hour we [apostles] hunger and thirst, we are ill-clad and buffeted and homeless, and we labour, working with our own hands (I Cor. 4.8,11).

Paul is drawing a contrast between the comfortable life of the Corinthians and the hard lot of the apostle. They are *stuffed* (Greek *kekoresmenoi*, sated), they have *become* rich; every day they are sitting down to square meals at church expense, and very likely enjoying better clothes donated by wealthier Christians. Meanwhile Paul often walks ten or fifteen miles from town to town, and may have nothing for his supper, and a hedge to protect him from the frost. They have given up working, and look to God for their meals; while he *labours, working with his own hands*. We notice the same phrase which came in I Thess. 4. There is some feeling behind his sarcasm.

As we read Paul, we tend to look down on the Petrines: they look a selfish and unrealistic lot, sitting there in comfort while the real Christian works his hands to the bone and suffers for it. So it will be good to listen for a moment to how the Petrines saw things:

> Do not lay up for yourselves treasures on earth, where moth and rust consume and where thieves break in and steal; but lay up for yourselves treasure in heaven, where neither moth nor rust consumes, and where thieves do not break in and steal. For where your treasure is, there will your heart be also. The eye is the lamp of the body. So, if your eye is generous, your whole body will be full of light . . . You cannot serve God and Mammon. Therefore I tell you, do not be anxious about your life, what you shall eat or what you shall drink, nor about your body, what you shall put on . . . Look at the birds of the air: they neither sow nor reap nor gather into barns, and yet your heavenly Father feeds them. Are you not of more value than they? . . . And why are you anxious about clothing? Consider the lilies of the field, how they grow; they neither toil nor spin; yet I tell you, even Solomon in all his glory was not arrayed like one of these (Matt. 6.19–29).

We should not allow Matthew's soaring eloquence to distract us from the uncompromising demands his religion makes on us. We are not to keep any savings (*Do not lay up for yourselves treasure on earth*); a deposit at the Halifax always ends in worldly concern (*where your treasure is, there will your heart be also*). Give the money away (*if your eye is generous, your whole body will be full of light* – Jews spoke of a generous or mean eye (Matt. 20.15) where we talk of a generous heart or a mean spirit); you have to choose between Christianity and money (*you cannot serve God and Mammon*). You don't need to be worried about the future if you do (*do not be anxious about your life*), and you do not need to earn money either (*look at the birds of the air: they neither sow nor reap, nor gather into barns . . . Consider the lilies of the field: they toil not, neither do they spin*). Work for the church, and keep the Law in the full form Jesus taught (*seek first his kingdom and his righteousness*), and God will supply all your needs (*all these things will be added unto you*). The word *toil* (Greek *kopian*) is the same word which Paul uses of his labours in I Cor. 4.12 and elsewhere. Petrine Christianity was a noble aspiration, not an excuse for selfish idleness; and Matthew's magnificent presentation of it has left a permanent question mark against the values of the acquisitive society.

The challenge to lay up treasure in heaven goes back to Jesus, for Mark tells the story of the rich man who asked him how to inherit eternal life. Jesus first enquired if he kept the Law, and then told him, 'One thing you lack; go, sell what you have, and give to the poor, and you will have *treasure in heaven*' (Mark 10.21). This is Petrine radicalism, and it is what the Jerusalem (and Thessalonian) Christians did – sold their property and gave it to the church for the benefit of poor fellow Christians. The only surprise is that we find it in Mark's Gospel, for Mark was a Pauline, and did not approve of such extreme measures.

Mark's dilemma may be illustrated by attendance at a modern church when Mark 10. 17–31 is the lesson for the day. What is the vicar to say? He could, of course, lean over the pulpit and say, 'The Lord's message is clear. Go after service, all of you, draw your money from the Building Society, sell any shares you have, put your homes on the market, and give it all to Christian Aid. You have Christ's promise that you will be looked after in this life; and you will have inflation-proof treasure in heaven'. The message is indeed clear, and if he said this, he would be entirely justified; but also he would have no congregation next week. Besides, people would say, 'What about you, vicar? What about selling your ropey old Ford?' So you are not very likely to hear a sermon like this. The vicar is more likely to say, 'Well now, this man had a problem about money . . .' Mark was in the same jam. The story was well-known in tradition, and it has the edifying effect of making ordinary Christians feel guilty at their half-heartedness; so he includes it. But then he adds that the disciples were astonished, saying, 'Who then can be saved?'; and Jesus gives the comforting conclusion, 'With men it is impossible; but *with God all things are possible*'. So all is well, brethren and sistren; even if you don't sell all you have, you can still have treasure in heaven.

Matthew is a Petrine, and I dare say he had given his own money away, but with time Petrines learned to be more cautious. The early enthusiasm flagged ('love will grow cold', Matt. 24.12), as Christ's promised return was postponed (the wicked servant in the parable says, 'My lord delays', Matt. 24.48); and Matthaean Christians took on an increasingly Anglican look. So when Matthew comes to Jesus' challenge to the rich young man, he has Jesus say, '*If you would be perfect*, go, sell what you possess and give to the poor' (Matt. 19.21). You see, brethren (Matthew was male-oriented), there are two levels of Christian. Some of us want to be *perfect*, and for them Christ poses this great challenge, and he offers the great reward. Others may be content to be second-class Christians; and they can be saved too. It was the same over sex. Some have gone the whole way, and made themselves eunuchs for the sake of the kingdom; but this is only for those who can receive it. The challenge to the apostles in the Sermon on the Mount was 'You therefore must be perfect, as your heavenly Father is perfect' (Matt. 5.48); other Christians heard the Sermon too (7.29), but perhaps they did not all feel the challenge to perfection. Here is the road down to Catholic mainstream Christianity: one standard for the 'religious', and perhaps the clergy, another for the laity.

Luke was in this respect more a straightforward Petrine than Matthew. He wrote the history of the early Jerusalem church in Acts, and he admired its whole-hearted generosity. So he writes, 'Blessed are the poor; for yours is the kingdom of God' (6.20); 'whoever of you does not renounce all that he has cannot be my disciple' (14.33).

Zacchaeus restores all his ill-gotten gains fourfold after giving half of his wealth to the poor (19.8). He cannot have had much left. The rich get short shrift in Luke (1.53; 6.24ff.; 16.14–31). Luke is the Gospel for Catholic Marxists and Liberation theologians.

11

The Ministry and the Church

Money led to trouble in other ways: for the two missions were divided on the question of whether their missionaries should earn their living, or should expect the local churches to provide for them. There was a long tradition in Palestine of holy men being looked after without charge: a rich woman in Shunem had fed Elisha in II Kings 4, and had built him 'a small roof chamber with walls', and a bed, a table, a chair and a lamp. One of the most certainly authentic of Jesus' directions was that his disciples should follow this precedent: Paul himself says, 'the Lord commanded that those who proclaim the gospel should get their living by the gospel' (I Cor. 9.14). Mark has Jesus send the twelve out two by two, directing them:

> to take nothing for their journey except a staff; no bread, no bag, no money in their belts, but wearing sandals; and not to put on two tunics. And he said to them, Where you enter a house, stay there until you leave the place (Mark 6.8–10).

The apostles were to travel light: just a staff to fend off dogs (and perhaps robbers); sandals, not shoes. They were to be entirely dependent on local hospitality, with no sandwiches nor money to buy a cup of tea, and no second tunic to give them protection from the night air if they had to sleep out. It must have added a certain piquancy to the venture.

Jesus' policy had two great advantages. First, it meant that the apostles had to put their trust in God. Their movement was based on the faith that God's kingdom had arrived, and that believers should share their resources for the common good: what was the use of expecting that from the ordinary Christian if the apostle did not exhibit the same trust? There certainly is something moving about a preacher who knows he will go without his supper and sleep *à la belle étoile* unless someone extends charity to him; there is no doubting his genuineness. Secondly, there is no better foundation for a church than the home of a kindly couple who have been persuaded by the preacher, and who invite their friends in to meet him. Paul himself built the Philippian church from the house of a woman whom he converted, a businesswoman called Lydia (Acts 16.14f.), and the Corinthian church from the house of Aquila and Priscilla (Acts 18.3).

Nevertheless, it was a policy with limits. Jews knew from the Law that they had a duty to care for the stranger in the land; and in Palestine, where the apostles and their followers evangelized, it must have been rare for anyone to go hungry and cold when on mission. But Paul was apostle to the Gentiles, who had no such charitable tradition. Distances in Palestine were not great, and the evangelist could probably depend on a bed and a meal in a Christian home not far away; Paul and Silas walked a thousand miles, or something near it, from Antioch to Troas, the length and breadth of modern Turkey, with often no Jewish population in the villages, let alone a Christian to welcome them. It was just impracticable to depend on local hospitality: Paul had tried – 'through many a sleepless night, in hunger and thirst, often without food, in cold and exposure' (II Cor. 11.27).

There was, however, a second Jewish tradition, which was that sages should earn their living with a trade, and Hillel for example had done this. Paul therefore made a practice of earning money wherever he settled from his skill as a leatherworker (Acts 18.2f.). This had its own advantages. First, he avoided giving the impression that he was sponging off the church; and second, he was giving an example of a Christian working, an example which was useful in a place where Christians were liable to give up their jobs and devote themselves to the kingdom. We saw this in Thessalonica: 'For you yourselves know how you ought to imitate us; we were not idle when we were with you, we did not eat anyone's bread without paying' (II Thess. 3.7f.). Of course in addition, there might be evangelistic opportunities while talking to customers.

Naturally, if unkindly, the Petrines turned this practice against Paul. When Jerusalem missionaries came to Corinth they said, 'You can see for yourselves that Paul is not a proper apostle. Jesus said that apostles were to be provided for by their converts. Paul pays for himself and works, because he is not an apostle.' This is a recurrent charge, and it evokes some indignation:

> Do we not have the right to our food and drink? Do we not have the right to be accompanied by a wife, as the other apostles and the brothers of the Lord and Cephas? . . . Nevertheless we have not made use of this right, but we endure anything rather than put an obstacle in the way of the gospel of Christ (I Cor. 9.4f., 12).

> Did I commit a sin in abasing myself so that you might be exalted, because I preached God's gospel without cost to you? I robbed other churches by accepting support from them in order to serve you (II Cor. 11.7f.).

It must have been very annoying to toil all day for a few shillings so as not to make yourself an incubus, and then be told this showed your claim to apostleship was bogus.

Paul's ministry survived this trouble, and in time his policy paid dividends. In every centre where he settled, he set up a committee to run the church after he left; normally the senior church members, 'those who are over you in the Lord' (I Thess. 5.12), who were spoken of as the *elders* (Greek *presbyteroi*, presbyters). Luke says that he sent for the elders of the Ephesian church to Miletus (Acts 20.17). One of these was chairman, perhaps usually the person in whose house the church met; we hear of one Archippus at Colosse who is told, 'See that you fulfil the ministry which you have received in the Lord' (Col. 4.17), and the church seems to be based in his home (Philemon 2). So there was a *local* ministry, and daughter churches grew out of local initiative. Epaphras was a convert of Paul's in Ephesus, but he came from Colosse, and it was he who took the gospel to his own home town, and to the neighbouring cities of Laodicea and Hierapolis (Col. 4.12f.). So the churches were strongly rooted locally, and with everyone working they were strong financially too.

By contrast the Jerusalem counter-mission was dependent upon 'wandering missionaries', who would set off in pairs from Palestine, with instructions to bring the Pauline churches to heel. This was not a good start, and it made a poor impression when it turned out that they expected to stay for weeks and perhaps months in some wretched family's home. The ever-charitable Pastor puts it like this:

> If anyone teaches otherwise and does not agree with the sound words of our Lord Jesus Christ and the teaching which accords with godliness, he is puffed up with conceit, he knows nothing . . . imagining that godliness is a means of gain . . . For the love of money is the root of all evils (I Tim. 6.3ff., 10).

In his view the Jewish-Christian counter-missionaries were in it for what they could get out of it; the fact that they expected to live off the churches made them sitting ducks for criticism.

We get a good insight into such counter-missionaries from the *Didache*, or *Teaching of the Twelve Apostles*, a short instruction by Paulines about 150 on how to run a church: the handbook was only discovered in 1887, and it gives a fine view of what the Petrines tried, and what they were up against:

> Whosoever therefore shall come and teach you all these things that have been said before, receive him; but if the teacher himself be perverted and teach a different doctrine to the destruction thereof, hear him not . . . But concerning the apostles and pro-phets, so do ye according to the ordinance of the Gospel. Let every apostle, when he cometh to you, be received as the Lord; but he shall not abide more than a single day, or if there be need, a second likewise; but if he abide three days, he is a false prophet. And when he departeth let the apostle receive nothing save bread, until he findeth shelter; but if he ask money he is a false prophet . . . And no prophet when he ordereth a table in the Spirit shall eat of it; otherwise he is a false prophet (*Didache* 11).

The new local Pauline pastor is liable to be put on the spot by the arrival of a couple of travelling teachers, who give themselves out to be *apostles*, that is emissaries of another church – perhaps a Palestinian, Petrine church – or *prophets*, that is with the gift of contact with the divine world. He is to be on his guard. (1) He is to listen carefully to their theology, and if it is not sound Pauline stuff, they are not to be let loose on the church at all (*hear him not*). (2) If they pass this test, they are to be *received* as Jesus expected (Mark 6.7ff.) – but with extreme caution. (3) One night is quite enough, or if they are totally exhausted two; but any suggestion of staying a third night proves them to be bogus. (4) When they go, give them a loaf apiece to keep them going till they reach the next town: any mention of money shows they are not genuine. (5) Be particularly wary of 'prophets' speaking in the Spirit. A well-known trick is to say that the Spirit or angel is telling the church to lay on a good spread. If that is claimed, prepare the dinner, and the 'prophet' can have the satisfaction of watching everyone else eat. One feels that Petrine missionaries would find this kind of reception rather depressing after a bit.

In this way the two missions built up very different images. It was not that Paul was any less authoritarian than the Jerusalem leadership; he was always putting his foot down when he could get away with it (II Thess. 3.14; I Cor. 5.3f.; 14.34ff.). But he was on his own, and he was forced to leave the running of the churches to local talent; whereas Jerusalem was the organized centre of a hierarchical Jewish church, as it was the organized centre of a hierarchical Judaism. So the Petrines thought in terms of decisions reached centrally and communicated by 'apostles and prophets', while Paul could only appeal and argue, and in the end trust his elders to act in the Spirit.

This difference shows itself in the way in which the two missions thought about the church. The most obvious idea of the church at first was that it was the *People of God*. God had chosen Israel from Abraham's days on, and formed himself a people; and this people had grown in faith and understanding over the centuries, through many rebellions and chastisements. Now, finally, God had acted through Jesus, and had brought in his kingdom. So Jesus had gone to 'the lost sheep of the house of Israel' (Matt. 15.24), and he had appointed twelve apostles for the twelve tribes of Israel; and the mission to Israel had at first been a dramatic success (Acts 2–5). With time all Israel would become Christian; and Paul's successes meant that there would even be Gentiles streaming in to join God's People.

We do find this idea in the New Testament. For instance I Peter says:

> But you [Christians] are a chosen race, a royal priesthood, a holy nation, God's own people . . . Once you were no people, but now you are God's people . . . (I Peter 2.9f.).

The phrases in the first verse are quoted from Ex. 19.5f., and those in the second from Hos. 2.23: both were addressed to Israel in the Old Testament, and are now applied to the church in the New Testament. But we hardly ever find this in Paul. Once, at the end of Galatians, where he has fought the principle of circumcision, he does pray peace and mercy 'upon the Israel of God' (6.16), as a kind of olive-branch; and once, when he is urging the Corinthians to expel faithless members, he appeals to the idea of a holy people with God indwelling it (II Cor. 6.16f.). But the whole idea raised uncomfortable questions. How did one become a member of God's people? By circumcision. No thank you. How did one remain a member? By keeping the Law. No thank you.

A second approach was to think of the church as a *Temple*. This idea was already suggested by the name which Jesus gave to Simon – *Cepha'*, Peter, Rock. Matthew understood this to mean that Peter was the foundation-stone on which the church was built, and the building image suggested the church as being like a temple (Matt. 16.18). When the Cephas group talked about this at Corinth, Paul replied hotly that 'like a skilled master builder I laid a *foundation* . . . no other foundation can any one lay than that which is laid, which is Jesus Christ' (I Cor. 3.10f.). He was not having the Petrines march away with his life's work, on the hollow claim that the foundation stone of the church was Peter: the foundation-stone was Jesus Christ, and him alone. We can see the Petrines using this Temple image also, from the fact that they referred to their leaders as the Pillars (Greek *styloi*). There were two famous pillars by Solomon's Temple, named Jachin and Boaz (I Kings 7.15–22).

Paul does not much care for the Temple image either, for this very reason: it embodied the suggestion of Petrine authority, the thing he was trying to get away from. A better image suggested itself from the experience which all Christians shared, of the Spirit. A spirit was what God breathed into Adam's clay body in Genesis, and the church could therefore be thought of as *the Body of Christ*, with the Holy Spirit as its animating force. Paul first speaks of the Body of Christ in I Cor. 12, where he is discussing the gifts of the Spirit; and he constantly returns to it, because it stresses the democratic element in Christianity. Everyone has got some gift, and we all display the fruit of the Spirit in our ethical lives. People who speak with tongues and heal depend on others who pay and organize; and even apostles and prophets are only like hands and feet to a body. Instead of stressing the authority of the leadership, the body image emphasizes the interdependence of all Christians, and the value of the least as well as the greatest. So Paul's favourite picture of the church, in Ephesians and Romans as well as in I Corinthians, is the Body of Christ.

But Paul is light on his feet, and he can use other people's images when they are convenient. He tells the errant Corinthians that their bodies are temples of the Holy Spirit, so fornication is unthinkable (I Cor. 6.19); later, when they have been eating meat which had been blessed in the name of a pagan god, he asks, 'What agreement has the temple of God with idols? For we are the temple of the living God (II Cor. 6.16). When visionary enthusiasts are trying to take over the Pauline church at Laodicea, near Colosse, Paul can adapt the old Petrine foundation claim to his own use:

> So then you are . . . built upon the foundation of the apostles and prophets, Christ Jesus himself being the headstone in whom the whole structure is joined together, and grows into a holy temple in the Lord; in whom you also are built into it for a dwelling place of God in the Spirit (Eph. 2.19–22).

These wild people – Petrines, again – must learn that they cannot rely on private experience only. Paul, now in his last years and more mellow and confident, appeals to the foundation idea as applying to the apostles generally (including himself, apostle to the Gentiles); in 3.5 they have become the *holy* apostles and prophets – the revelation came to them, and they are the basis of the church. What about Jesus Christ then? Well, the church is a *growing* building, and each Christian is a stone in it; and Paul, with his lively imagination, pictures Christ as the *keystone* on the top of the arch, which holds the whole thing together. You cannot but admire the apostle. Eighteen centuries before Disraeli, he perfected the art of stealing the opposition's clothes while they were bathing.

12

The Phasing of the Future

The Petrines' *already* view of the kingdom was a menace to Paul: it put the whole mission in jeopardy. All the talk about tongues and visions was so inward-looking; the high ascetic line on sex, marriage and divorce was unrealistic and could not last; it was too easy to give up work and consider the lilies of the field. The impression all this gave to outsiders was of a lot of idle layabouts full of talk; and quite soon one and then another was falling into sexual temptation. It must be stopped.

Early in his mission Paul tried a line of attack which he was not to repeat, but which became a standard approach to his successors. Here is an excerpt from II Thess. 2, written about 51:

Now concerning the coming of our Lord Jesus Christ and our assembling to meet him, we beg you, brethren, not to be quickly shaken in mind or excited, either by spirit or by word, or by letter purporting to be from us, to the effect that the day of the Lord has come. Let no one deceive you in any way; for that day will not come, unless the rebellion comes first, and the man of lawlessness is revealed, the son of perdition, who opposes and exalts himself against every so-called god or object of worship, so that he takes his seat in the temple of God, proclaiming himself to be God. Do you not remember that when I was still with you I told you this? And you know what is restraining him now so that he may be revealed in his time. For the mystery of lawlessness is already at work; only he who now restrains it will do so until he is out of the way. And then the lawless one will be revealed, and the Lord Jesus will slay him with the breath of his mouth and destroy him by his appearing and his coming (2.1–8).

Paul is concerned that a damaging heresy (*let no one deceive you*, cf. 2.9–12) has upset (*shaken in mind, excited*) his Thessalonian converts. It was the view which we have met in I Cor. 4, that the kingdom had already come (*to the effect that the day of the Lord has come*). The idea has gained force in three ways: Christians cry it out during services in moments of ecstasy (*by spirit*); they appeal to the Bible (*by word*), perhaps especially Malachi 4.5, 'Behold, I will send you Elijah the prophet before the great and terrible *day of the Lord comes*'; and a *letter* has been received claiming to be from Paul. As forging would be a problem in a little group of churches where the letters were carried by well-known church figures like Timothy, we have to think of another explanation. I have mentioned above (ch.9) that Silas, Paul's co-missionary, was a Jerusalem Christian, and Paul says he *told them this when he was still with them*, so the teaching was probably Silas'; and just as Paul starts his letter, 'Paul, Silvanus and Timothy . . .' (1.1), so perhaps Silas started his, 'Silvanus, Paul and Timothy'.

Paul answers the *already* view by setting out three *phases* which comprise present and future history. (1) *Now* is a time of pause. *The mystery of lawlessness is already at work*, that is, the world is full of cruelty, oppression and disobedience of God's Law; and especially perhaps there is persecution of the church, which was the topic of II Thess. 1. But something, indeed someone, is holding up the advance into phase 2: *you know what is restraining him, he who now restrains it* – the nature of this restraining power is unexplained. (2) *Next* will come the *revealing of the man of lawlessness, the son of perdition*. He will be a terrifying and blasphemous figure, who will *proclaim himself to be God, and take his seat in the temple of God*. Things will reach an all-time low under him, marked by *the activity of Satan with all power and pretended signs and wonders* (2.9). (3) *Finally*, he will be *destroyed, at the coming of our Lord Jesus*; and after that things will be fine. So it is a hopeless mistake to speak of *the day of the Lord having come* (this is, in fact, *a strong delusion sent by God*, 2.11); it cannot come until phase 3, and we are still in phase 1.

The amazed modern reader asks himself, Where on earth did all this come from? How can Paul be so sure?: and the answer is, He got it from the Bible. The book of Daniel reads like a detailed prophecy of the future, and Paul knows Daniel better than we do.

Daniel has in fact made use of a simple technique. The book was written in the 160s BC, when the Greek king Antiochus IV persecuted the Jews; he gave himself the name Epiphanes, God manifest, and desecrated the Temple, where he set up an altar to Zeus. Our Daniel was written as if by one Daniel who lived under King Nebuchadnezzar, four hundred years earlier; and so he is able to 'prophesy' a whole lot of things which had actually already happened. This certainly gives the reader confidence that his prophecies are by divine inspiration, and then it is easy to be encouraged, and to believe his real prophecies, which are that the end is just ahead.

In the first half of the book the Jews are persecuted: their leaders are thrown into burning fiery furnaces, dens of lions, etc. Then in ch. 9 Daniel makes a great confession, 'All Israel has transgressed thy law . . .' (9.11); and the angel Gabriel comes to explain what is happening. He and Michael, Israel's own 'prince' (angel), are pressing God's purposes on; but 'the prince of the kingdom of Persia withstood me twenty-one days . . . now I will return to fight with the prince of Persia; and when I am through with him, lo, the prince of Greece will come' (10.13,20). In ch. 11 the 'prince' of Greece does come, bringing a terrible Greek king (Antiochus). He stops the Temple sacrifice, and sets up 'the abomination of desolation' there (11.31). 'He shall exalt himself and magnify himself above every god, and shall speak astonishing things against the God of gods' (11.36). He will be destroyed (11.45); and then 'many of those who sleep in the dust of the earth shall awake' – that is, the resurrection of the dead will take place (12.2).

Paul reads all this as a prophecy of his own days. The persecutions of the saints, the *lawlessness* of Israel, the activity of mysterious 'princes' in heaven *restraining* the advance of God's purposes *until they are out of the way* – all this is understood as phase 1, *Now*; it is the events which Paul sees in front of his eyes. But we have not yet reached phase 2, described in Dan. 11, where the blasphemous king will *exalt himself against every so-called god or object of worship, so that he takes his seat in the Temple of God, proclaiming himself to be God*. This was a perfectly real expectation because it was only ten years before that the mad Roman emperor Caligula had ordered his statue to be erected in the Jerusalem Temple, and fortunately he had died before the order was carried out (41). Finally phase 3 would come, as foretold in Dan. 12, with the resurrection of the dead, *the coming of our Lord Jesus Christ and our assembling to meet him*, live and dead Christians together. The blasphemous king would be killed, and God's kingdom would come. The whole picture is extremely satisfying to a Pauline, because it follows the sequence of the Book of Daniel from start to finish (with suitable selections); and it proves quite conclusively that it is a *deceit* and a *delusion* to say that the kingdom/day of the Lord is here *already*. On the contrary, God's word shows that we are only in phase 1; we have the terrible phase 2 to go through yet before the Lord comes in phase 3.

Paul found other matters to contest in his later letters, but the problem of the *already* view did not go away, and we find Mark fighting it twenty years later. Mark devotes a whole chapter, ch. 13, to a prophecy by Jesus of the future; and according to Mark, Jesus saw the future as divided into three phases! According to him, too, Jesus was particularly anxious that people should not get hold of the wrong end of the stick, just like Paul! He begins the prophecy, 'Take heed that no one *leads you astray*' (13.5). Of the opening trials he says, '*do not be excited*: this must take place, but the end is not yet' (13.7); and when he has gone through them he concludes, 'this is but the beginning of birth pangs' (13.8). Both the thought and the language are close to Thessalonians, and we have found Mark to be a good Pauline in many other matters.

The phases are clearly indicated, by these and other markers. Phase (1) runs from 13.5 to 13.13, and consists of general troubles – wars, earthquakes, famines, etc. – and of persecutions of the church (13.9–13). These things are the beginning of birth-pangs [phase 1], and the end [phase 3] is not yet. With 13.14 comes another marker: '*But* when you see the abomination of desolation . . . *then* let those who are in Judaea flee to the mountains'. Phase 2 is coming with the fulfilment of Dan. 11.31 on the abomination of desolation, and at that point Christians will have to flee; and there will be further dangers of false prophets 'leading astray, if possible, the elect' (13.22). The prophecy of phase 2 ends, 'But take heed; I have told you all these things beforehand' (13.23); and phase 3 is then signalled, '*But in those days, after that tribulation*, the sun will be darkened . . . And *then* they will see the Son of Man coming' (13.24ff.).

Mark knows that the Book of Daniel is the place to go for the details, and he fills in some of the blanks from the same source which had stood Paul in good stead. 'These things must happen' comes in Dan. 2.28, and kingdoms rise against kingdoms in Dan. 2.39. 'He who endures' comes in Dan. 12.12 (Greek), and the time of tribulation such as never has been since creation in Dan. 12.1. The shortening of the days from a week to half a week ('a time and two times and half a time' (i.e. 3 ½ years)/1290 days) comes in Dan. 7.25 and 12.12, and the coming of the Son of Man on the clouds of heaven is drawn from Dan. 7.13. There are some other prophecies referred to, but the main structure of Mark 13 is primarily dependent on Daniel.

The only section of the chapter which does not have a lot of Daniel and Thessalonians behind it is the persecution paragraph, 13.9–13; and here the details are strongly reminiscent of Paul and his friends. 'You will be beaten in synagogues' reminds us of II Cor. 11.24, 'Five times I have received of the Jews forty lashes save one'. 'You will stand before governors and kings' speaks especially of Paul, because he is the only Christian to be tried before governors (Felix and Festus) and a king (Herod Agrippa II) in Acts (23–26). 'The gospel must first be preached to all nations' reflects Paul's personal mission. The promise of the Holy Spirit to Christians at their trials is evidenced in the eloquence of Stephen (Acts 7), and Paul in numerous speeches. 'Brother shall deliver up brother to death' may also be an echo of Paul's martyrdom, for I Clement 5 (supposedly written in the 90s) says that Paul's death was caused by [Christian] *envy*. Whereas the Jerusalem Christians were generally in good repute with pious Jews, it might very well have been said of Paulines, 'you will be hated by all men for my name's sake'.

The cumulative effect of these parallels is to suggest strongly that Mark has little or no tradition of what Jesus actually said about the future. He has a tradition, and it is the Pauline tradition, embattled with the Petrine *already* doctrine. That tradition affirmed robustly that the kingdom could not have come yet, because scripture said not. Daniel had laid out three phases, and we were still securely in phase 1. Mark amplifies that tradition, and ascribes it to the Lord himself, as is apparently implied by I Thess. 4.15, 'this we declare to you by a word of the Lord'; he takes the amplifications from scripture, and especially from Daniel, and for the persecution section he has the history of his own hero to draw on. But for Mark there has been one all-significant step forward. He had just lived through the desecration of the Temple at the end of the Jewish War; so any moment now Christians would *see the abomination of desolation set up where he ought not* (13.14). Phase 2 was about to begin: *let the reader understand.*

As is well known, prophesying is a dangerous profession, and the difficulties arise when a prophecy is not fulfilled. We have an interesting example of how to cope with this problem in the writing of another Pauline, the seer John in Revelation. For Revelation is in a way an extended form of Mark 13: it is an outline of history and history-to-come, set out in imagery of unsurpassed splendour, and it falls into four phases. It is possible to pick these out without much hesitation, because before each phase the Seer describes a scene of worship in heaven which is to inaugurate the new movement. After the opening Letters we have a vision of the Divine Throne, and of the Lamb who comes to open the Seven Seals (4–5). Then, after a series of woes, we have a second passage in heaven: the Seventh Trumpet is blown, and the coming of the kingdom is announced (11.15–19); the Woman is seen in heaven, and there is war in heaven between Michael and Satan (12). After the appearance of the Beast (13), and other matters, there is a third heavenly section as the angels take the Seven Bowls full of the wrath of God (15). Finally in 19 the great multitude in heaven cry Hallelujah, and Christ rides forth on the white horse for the Last Judgment.

It is not difficult to align these phases with those in Mark 13. Rev 6, after the opening heavenly scene, is widely understood to correspond to Mark's phase 1. The four Horsemen symbolize war and famine and death, and there is an earthquake, as in Mark 13.7f. After the second scene in heaven we have the Beast, with his blasphemies, and men worshipping him, and his oppression of the church: here is the Man of Lawlessness of II Thess. 2, the abomination of desolation of Dan. 11 and Mark 13.14, and the events of phase 2. After the third scene of heavenly worship come the Bowls which strike the elements: there is blood and darkness and the sun is smitten, as in phase 3, Mark 13.24f. Finally Christ's riding forth on the White Horse and the resurrection of the dead to judgment correspond to the second part of Mark's phase 3, the coming of the son of Man. The Seer has just split the third phase into (a) the signs in heaven, and (b) Christ's Coming.

But there is a twist to all this. Just as phase 3 has been divided into 3a and 3b, so has phase 1: for the Seven Seals are followed by Seven Trumpets, and there is a gap between them, a small gap (8.1), silence in heaven, about the space of half an hour. There follow a series of woes which bear a marked resemblance to events which took place in the 70s. We hear of a terrifying comet in 73, like the great star which fell from heaven (8.10f.). In 79 came the famous eruption of Vesuvius, when one third of the volcano blew into the sky and mostly came down in the sea, like the great mountain, burning with fire, which was thrown into the sea in 8.8f. The red-hot pumice descended on the hapless inhabitants of Pompeii, like the smoke which came up from the pit, and the locusts which tormented mankind in 9.1–6. In 80 the rumour went round that Nero had risen from the dead, and was leading the armies of Parthian cavalry from across the Euphrates (for these details cf. Suetonius on the Life of Titus); like the cavalry released on the Euphrates in 9.13–19.

Why has the Seer intruded his phase 1b in Rev. 8–9? Because Mark had taken the story up to 70, and the oppression of the Beast had not taken place under Vespasian (69–79). The Seer thinks that Titus (79–81) is the successor to Nero, and so the Second Beast (13.11–18). So he has a ten-year gap to fill; and surely, to anyone living through the eruption of Vesuvius, it must have seemed that the gods were in dire and wrathful action. So only half an hour separates the Trumpets from the Seals; and the Trumpets are the dread events of the 70s. In this way the Lord's prophecy of the end of history in Mark 13 is subtly extended by a decade: so subtly that the Seer's handiwork has hardly been noticed from that day to this.

13

The Spirit as the Brake of the Church

The tension between the two missions was most difficult to resolve over the Holy Spirit. On the Petrine side there was sustained excitement over the tongues, the visions, the revelations, the healings, the miracles and the rest: in a society wracked by poverty, sickness and deprivation, the arrival of the kingdom was indeed good news, and Saturday nights at the church supper were a time of marvellous transport into a happier world. Paul was nervous at the excesses and unreality of much of this; but he believed in the Spirit too, and accepted the genuineness of the experience. He just wanted workaday gifts like administration and the provision of resources given their place, and the primacy accorded to the *fruit* of the Spirit, the ethical elements of love, joy, peace and so on.

As time went by, the tension became apparent within the Pauline wing itself. Mark hardly mentions the Spirit once it has descended into Jesus at the baptism. There is the sin against the Holy Spirit in 3.28ff., which Mark interprets as committed by the scribes who saw Jesus casting out demons and said he did it by Beelzebul, the prince of demons. In 13.11 the apostles are promised that when they are put on trial, they need not be anxious what to say, for the Holy Spirit will speak for them. That is it. One does not get the impression that St Mark would feel at home in a Pentecostal church today.

But Luke, as so often, is there to bridge the gap. His work is dominated by the Holy Spirit, which acts as the initiator of the gospel and the engine of the church. In the Old Testament the Spirit was spoken of rather rarely, coming upon certain prophets and holy men. With the beginning of Luke's Gospel, it is like a thunderstorm. John is to be filled with the Spirit (1.15); the Holy Spirit is to come upon Mary for the conception of Jesus (1.35); Elizabeth is filled with the

Holy Spirit and prophesies when Mary visits her (1.41); Zechariah is filled with the Holy Spirit and delivers the Benedictus (1.67); the Holy Spirit is upon Simeon in the Temple (2.26f.). Finally the Holy Spirit descends upon Jesus himself at his Baptism (3.22); full of the Holy Spirit, he is led by the Spirit into the desert for his temptation (4.1); he returns in the power of the Spirit into Galilee (4.14), and preaches his famous opening sermon at Nazareth on the text, 'The Spirit of the Lord is upon me' (4.18; Isa. 61.1).

Luke views history as like an old-fashioned hour-glass. Jesus is the funnel. Before him the Spirit acted occasionally through the prophets, dramatically and frequently around his birth. During his ministry the Spirit's action is concentrated in him; and especially in his 'preaching good tidings to the poor . . . proclaiming release to the captives . . . proclaiming the acceptable year of the Lord' (4.18f.). After the resurrection the disciples are told to wait in Jerusalem for God's promise (24.49), and in Acts 2 the Spirit comes on them in tongues of fire, like a rushing mighty wind. Every phase of the church's life is then presided over by the Spirit, which indwells the church. When Ananias and his wife try to deceive Peter about the amount of money they received for their land, they have tempted the Spirit of the Lord (Acts 5.9); the Holy Spirit witnesses through Peter (5.32). Stephen and Philip and the others of the Seven are men full of the Spirit (6.3), and the Spirit in Stephen is irresistible (6.10). The Spirit of the Lord catches up Philip and he is found at Azotus (8.39f.); he falls upon Cornelius and his company at Joppa (10.44); he commands the setting apart of Barnabas and Saul for the great Gentile mission (13.2); and there are many references to his activity throughout Acts. Once Jesus is risen, the Spirit is poured forth on the church for its great work (2.33): now the sand is pouring through the hour-glass as it never did before the Lord's coming.

When we examine these texts, though, we find that the action of the Spirit is much more limited than it was on both sides in I Corinthians. The most common activity of the Spirit is in *prophesying* (that is, delivering inspired messages from God), *preaching, and defending oneself in court*. Luke sees the Spirit as mainly exercised in proclaiming the gospel through his chosen servants. A second activity is in *speaking with tongues* (foreign languages, as Luke understands it in Acts 2); but here the action is extremely limited – it happens only four times, at four crucial moments in the history of the church. The first Christians speak with tongues when the Spirit comes at Pentecost to start the church (Acts 2.1–13); the first non-Jewish Christians (Samaritans) can be seen to have received the Spirit, and so may be presumed to be speaking with tongues (Acts 8.14–18); the Spirit falls on Cornelius' party, the first fully Gentile Christians, causing them to speak with tongues (10.44ff.); and twelve Gentiles at Ephesus who had received only John's baptism, speak with tongues when Paul baptizes them (19.1–7).

This may be held to be *rather* Pauline; and Luke was a disciple of Paul. That is to say, Paul thought prophecy was the most important activity of the Spirit (I Cor. 14), and tongues the least; and Luke's account chimes in with this. It is difficult to be sure, because as soon as the spirit is given in Acts 2 we hear of the sharing of goods, devout prayer, joy, etc., and then the healing of a lame man (Acts 3); and it could be that Luke is thinking of all these things as the effects of the Spirit's coming. But he does not speak of the Spirit as active in healings: rather it is 'Jesus Christ' (9.34), or 'his name' (3.16), or 'God was with [Jesus]' (10.38). We rather get the impression that Luke is not too keen to associate healings with the Spirit because that was something the *Petrines* stressed, and reproached Paul with his failure to heal much (II Cor. 12.12). In any case the central emphasis is on the power to proclaim the gospel: that is the thing normally done by those who are 'full of the Holy Spirit'.

This limiting of the action of the Spirit is carried much further by *John*. In John the Holy Spirit appears in four activities.

1. Jesus says to Nicodemus, 'unless one is born of water and the Spirit, he cannot enter the kingdom of God. That which is born of the flesh is flesh, and that which is born of the Spirit is Spirit' (John 3.5f.). That is, *the Spirit is given at baptism.* Jewish Christians like Nicodemus, Petrines, thought that they had become God's people by *circumcision*, by being Jews; but that is a total error, that is depending on being *born of the flesh* as Jews, and that can affect only *the flesh.* Furthermore the Petrine idea that baptism automatically made a Jew *spiritual*, and so enabled him at once to *enter the kingdom of God* here on earth, was a piece of odious arrogance. No, baptism meant being *born again, from above*: it was a completely new start, and

that is what proud Jewish Christians like Nicodemus need to realize. That is the only way even to *see the kingdom of God*, let alone *enter* it. A humble Gentile Christian who is baptized is thereby *born of water* (in which he/she is immersed) *and the Spirit* (which he/she receives as an invisible gift).

John does not think much of speaking with tongues. He goes on: 'The Spirit/wind (they are the same word *pneuma* in Greek) blows where it wills, and you hear the sound of it, but you do not know whence it comes or whither it goes; so it is with everyone who is born of the Spirit' (3.8). The spirit is not limited to those of Jewish birth at all: it *blows where it wills*, and the big growth in the Church has proved to be among the Gentile communities. Many Christians of all kinds (*everyone who is born of the Spirit*) have experienced the Spirit as like a *rushing, mighty wind*, and they have *heard the sound of it* (Greek *phonen*, his voice) in the 'tongues' which occur in worship; but Petrines (*you*) do not understand it, they *do not know whence it comes or whither it goes*. John is a strongly contentious Gospel, and the movement that the contention is against is the Petrine mission. Nicodemus was probably a successful Petrine missionary who had followers in John's church at Ephesus, and John is putting them in their place.

The idea that every Christian received the Holy Spirit when he was baptized goes back to Paul. Baptism was a big moment, often prepared for by a period of fasting by the whole church (*Didache* 7), and when the new Christian came up from the water, he/she often shouted out 'Abba' (Father) in an experience of release. Paul says:

> For you did not receive the Spirit of slavery to fall back into fear, but you have received the Spirit of sonship. When we cry Abba!, Father!, it is the Spirit himself bearing witness with our Spirit that we are children of God (Rom. 8.15f.).

The new Christian felt assured that he had become a child of God. In the same way John writes:

> Jesus stood up and cried, If anyone thirst, let him come to me and drink. He who believes in me, as the scripture has said, Out of his belly shall flow rivers of living water. Now this he said about the

Spirit, which those who believed in him were to receive; for as yet the Spirit had not been given, because Jesus was not yet glorified (John 7.37ff.).

Jesus *cries*, like the new-born Christian who *cries Abba!* in Rom. 8 – that is, he is inspired. He calls to everyone who feels the need for God, *anyone who thirsts*, and offers them satisfaction in abundance, *rivers of living water*. John has adapted a text from scripture, Zech. 14.8, and when he writes *Out of his belly*, he means Jesus': 'his' without a person mentioned before often refers to Jesus. So this spiritual satisfaction is what John thinks of as the primary result of conversion and baptism (*he who believes in me*), and he agrees with Luke's picture of the hour-glass when he says that *the Spirit has not been given, because Jesus was not yet glorified* – not yet crucified, resurrected and taken to heaven.

2. We have already met the Petrines trying to influence Pauline converts. Sometimes they sent emissaries out in pairs to call on Pauline churches: they did this at Antioch (ch. 1: Gal. 2.1–14), and later in the Galatian churches (Galatians, often), and we found it still going on a century later in *Didache* 11. Sometimes they received convenient messages from angels (Col. 2.16ff.) or spirits (I Cor. 12.1–3). Paulines resisted this, as well they might. John writes about the 'anointing' which Christians receive at baptism: 'the anointing which you received from him abides in you, and you have no need that anyone should teach you; as his anointing teaches you about everything, and is true and is no lie, abide in him' (I John 2.27). You had a good course of instruction which I gave you when you were baptized (*anointed*), and this *anointing teaches you about everything and is true*; so pay no attention to any other teachers who may visit you – *you have no need that anyone should teach you* – and simply *abide in him*.

We find the same message in the Gospel:

But the Advocate, the Holy Spirit, whom the Father will send in my name, he will teach you all things, and bring to remembrance all that I have said to you. (John 14.26).

When the Spirit of truth comes, he will guide you into all the truth; for he will not speak on his own authority, but whatever he hears he will speak, and he will declare to you the things that are to come. He will glorify me, for he will take what is mine and declare it to you (John 16.13f.).

The Spirit is now *the brake on the church*. He will not produce anything new. He will be sent in *Jesus' name*, and he will merely *bring to remembrance all that Jesus said* – i.e. He will reinforce the message of John's Gospel. He will not produce new teachings *on his own authority*, the kind of stuff the Petrines are always pushing: it will only be *what is mine*, Jesus' teachings. One particularly important side of Jesus' teachings, which had been developed in the Pauline churches (ch. 12) was the phasing of the future, *the things that are to come*.

3. In 15.18–16.11 the disciples are warned of persecutions they will suffer: they will be hated, expelled from the synagogue, and sometimes martyred. The particular scene envisaged is the synagogue, where they will be accused:

> But when the Advocate comes, whom I shall send to you from the Father, even the Spirit of truth, who proceeds from the Father, he will bear witness to me; and you also are witnesses, because you have been with me from the beginning (15.26f.). And when [the Advocate] comes, he will convict the world concerning sin and righteousness and judgment: concerning sin, because they do not believe in me; concerning justification, because I go to the Father, and you will see me no more; concerning judgment because the prince of this world is judged (16.7–11).

The language is all from the law-court. Christians are on trial as law-breakers, and they are to be *witnesses* to their faith; those who accuse them will be *convicted* (Greek *elenchein*, to cross-question and prove wrong). The accusation is that the Christians have *sinned*, that is, broken the Law; but the real sin will be shown to be Jewish refusal to *believe in Jesus*. Jews will claim that *justification* before God is for those who keep the Law; but God has shown whom he justifies by resurrecting Jesus to *go to the Father*. They sit in *judgment* on Christians, but by the cross and the resurrection God has *judged the prince of this world*, the devil, and the Jews who are his children (8.44).

How will quiet, modest Christians, with no experience at all of public speaking, be able to achieve such an effect? They cannot do it themselves; they will rise to heights of simple eloquence through the Holy Spirit, who (as in Mark 13.11) will teach them. John uses the curious word often translated *Paraclete*, which I have rendered *Advocate*: *para* means *to* (Latin *ad*), *kletos* means *called* (Latin *vocatus*), and Tertullian, a century after John, uses this translation, *advocatus*, a barrister. The context shows that he is right. The Holy Spirit is our barrister, who will inspire us to confound our accusers in the hour of need.

4. After the resurrection, Jesus comes to the Twelve in the evening and he says,

> Peace be with you. As the Father has sent me, even so I send you. And when he had said this, he breathed on them, and said to them, Receive the Holy Spirit. If you forgive the sins of any, they are forgiven; if you retain the sins of any, they are retained.

This is, I suppose, the most disappointing passage in the Bible. Jesus has risen from the dead, and he comes to his apostles, and with enormous power and simplicity passes on to them his own commission: he had been *sent* by God, now they are *sent* in turn. To empower them for their task, *he breathes on them, and says, Receive the Holy Spirit*. The ancient listener will catch two echoes: God *breathed into Adam the breath of life, and Adam became a living soul*; and Ezekiel saw the valley of dry bones, and was told to prophesy to the Spirit, and the Spirit breathed life into the dead (Ezek. 37). So here, he feels, is the moment of new life: as God brought life into man in Adam, and restored life through Ezekiel, so now there is a new miracle, a new living organism has come into being, the church. And does Jesus say, 'Go into the world; carry the gospel to all men; face persecution; the blood of the martyrs is the seed of the Church?' No: he give them *authority* to distinguish genuine from false repentance – the means to *control* the organization. I can see the Holy Catholic Church coming round the mountain.

The Paulines were frightened of the Spirit, and by degrees they domesticated it. Paul exalted the workaday gifts and the ethical fruits over the spectacular but dangerous ecstatic gifts. Luke retained its power as the engine of the church's mission, the force behind its preaching and the (very) occasional miracle of tongues. For Mark it has virtually disappeared. For John it is what makes you a Christian, and if you should be accused, it will give you great power of speech; but in practice it will be limited to reminding you of Jesus' words which you have been taught already, and it will enable the clergy to keep the show on the right lines.

14

The Messiah Christology

The Petrines and the Paulines were divided over many practical matters, which I have now outlined; but the serious divisions, the ones that were to end in charges of heresy and in excommunication, were over doctrine. The most acute doctrinal question was the simple one, Who was Jesus?; and attempts to answer this question have a technical name which it is convenient for the reader to become familiar with: they are called christologies.

The most obvious answer to the question was the one offered by Peter, which was briefly discussed in ch. 3 above: Peter said, 'You are *the Christ*'. *Christos* is a Greek word meaning *Anointed*, and is the translation of the Hebrew word *Mashiah*, usually Anglicized as Messiah. The Israelites, like the English, used to anoint their kings, and it was felt that this anointing consecrated them. Saul was anointed king by Samuel, and David felt that he should not 'touch the Lord's Anointed'; the phrase has been carried over into the eighteenth century song, 'The Vicar of Bray' – 'And damn'd be he who dare resist Or touch the Lord's Anointed'. In the course of time David was himself anointed king, and God promised that there would never fail one of David's line to sit on his throne, for ever; God would punish any national disobedience, but he would never take away the kingship from David's dynasty, in perpetuity (II Sam. 7.14). The word Messiah is used occasionally in the Old Testament for the Israelite king. In Ps. 2 the heathen nations are said to rise up 'against the LORD and against His Anointed'; and when Israel was in exile, the prophet could even speak of the Persian king Cyrus as '[God's] Anointed' (Isa. 45.1).

David son of Jesse and his descendants ruled in Jerusalem for more than four centuries, from 1000 BC to 586; but then the city was captured by the Babylonians, the last king, Zedekiah, died in exile, and there were no more kings of Israel. This did not stop the Jews from believing God's promises, and in dark days it could be prophesied:

> There shall come forth a shoot from the stump of Jesse, and a branch shall grown out of his roots (Isa. 11.1).

By the end of the old era this hope came to be expressed in the form that God would soon send 'Lord Messiah' (Psalms of Solomon, 17.32). Other people than kings were anointed, including High Priests, and it was possible to speak of a High Priest as a Messiah too: in the Dead Sea Scrolls there is an expectation of the coming of *two Messiahs*, a Messiah of Aaron – a High Priestly Messiah – and a Messiah of Israel. But in later Jewish writings 'the Messiah' is the expected king, of the line of David; and this is the sense which underlies the New Testament.

This straightforward use is common. Blind Bartimaeus addresses Jesus, 'Son of David, pity me!' (Mark 10.47f.), to everyone's amazement; and as Jesus enters Jerusalem the crowd cries, 'Hosanna! Blessed be the coming kingdom of our father David!' (Mark 11.9f.). The angel Gabriel says of Jesus to Mary, 'The Lord will give him the throne of his father David' (Luke 1.32). If Jesus is the *son of David*, then to Christians that means he is *the Christ*. It is obviously an important moment in Mark's Gospel when Peter says, 'You are the Christ', even if Mark thinks that is only part of the truth (Mark 8.29). We cannot be sure if Peter said this during Jesus' lifetime: some later insights were afterwards read back into the time of the ministry, and it has often been suspected that Peter tumbled to this only after Jesus' death and resurrection. But in any case all Christians accepted that this was a true insight, and this was so in a matter of a few years: within a decade we hear that the disciples who fled to Antioch were there called Christians (Messianists, Acts 11.26).

Paul himself accepted this meaning. He speaks of:

> the gospel concerning [God's] Son, who came to be from the seed of David according to the flesh, and was designated Son of God

according to the Spirit of holiness by his resurrection from the dead, Jesus Christ our Lord (Rom. 1.3f.).

Paul thinks (as we know from many other texts) that Jesus Christ was *God's Son* from eternity, but he was 'born of a woman' (Gal. 4.4), and that means he must have been conceived. Paul knows nothing of the virginal conception which we find in Matthew and Luke, and he thinks that Jesus was conceived (*came to be*, Greek *genomenou*) from a human father, Joseph, who was descended from (*from the seed of) David according to the flesh*. In this way he is Jesus *Christ*, and he fulfils the promise in scripture that God would send a king of David's line. There is nothing peculiar, in Jewish eyes, in the notion of Jesus' twofold sonship, son of David (via Joseph) *according to the flesh*, Son of God *according to the Spirit of holiness*. For in days of old the psalmist had hailed God's decree as proclaiming to the Davidic King in Jerusalem, 'You are my Son: today I have begotten you' (Ps. 2.7). The King had been born twenty years or whenever before, the son of the previous King; now, at his coronation, he had become God's *Son* – we should say adopted, but they said *begotten*. In the same way Jesus was *designated Son of God by the resurrection from the dead*. Jesus rose again, and had been enthroned Son of God in heaven.

We meet the dual sonship again in Luke's writing. In Luke 1–2 the evangelist makes it quite clear that he thinks that Mary was a virgin mother, and that Jesus' conception was from the Holy Spirit, and not from Joseph. But at the same time he can put a sermon in Paul's mouth in which it is said:

> [God] raised up David to be their king . . . Of this man's seed God has brought to Israel a Saviour, Jesus, as he promised . . . What God promised to the fathers, this he has fulfilled to us their children by raising Jesus; as also it is written in the second psalm, Thou art my Son, today I have begotten thee (Acts 13.22f., 32f.).

Luke has carried over the Pauline teaching of Rom. 1.3f.: Jesus' literal, human descent from David, and his designation as God's Son by the resurrection, citing Ps. 2.7 for the purpose.

People sometimes wish to think that the human descent came through Mary rather than through Joseph; but it should be noticed that this is excluded by the use of the phrase *from the seed of David* in both passages. While we lack any clear statement of accepted Jewish understandings of human generation at the time, the language seems to imply the so-called flower-pot theory. Just as you may go into your greenhouse in April, and fill a flower-pot with John Innes No. 1 compost, and push into it say a courgette seed; and then a fortnight later see a marvellous green shoot springing from the surface: so may a man sow his seed in his wife, and then a few months later see signs of the marvel of human conception. The life was latent in the courgette *seed*; the compost was simply the means for its growth. In the same way the Jews spoke as if the life of the child was latent in the seed of the father; the mother merely gave the means of growth, like the flower-pot. Jesus *came to be from the seed of David*: he was the son of the son of the son of . . . a long line of *fathers* going back ultimately to David, *according to the flesh*.

The Paulines hung on to the Messiah christology despite the contradiction that I have just pointed to in Luke (Jesus could not *both* be descended from David and *also* be the Son of God through the overshadowing of a virgin mother by the Holy Spirit). It was the only proper way to give sense to the title *Christ*, and it implied a claim which the Paulines wished to make, that Jesus was the fulfilment of many promises in the Old Testament. So the Pastor writes, 'Remember Jesus Christ, risen from the dead, from the seed of David, as preached in my gospel' (II Tim. 2.8); and the Pauline Ignatius can write unashamedly, 'For our God, Jesus the Christ, was conceived in the womb of Mary according to a dispensation, of the seed of David but also of the Holy Ghost' (Ephes. 18). Modern Christians too may sometimes sing, slightly mystified, of Jesus as 'the stem of Jesse's rod'.

Matthew, as we have repeatedly seen, was sympathetic to the Petrine mission, and Luke wished to reconcile the two movements; but they would not have got their Gospels into the New Testament if they had not been (nearly) orthodox on the central doctrinal question. Paulines thought Jesus was *the Son of God* in a much stronger sense, they thought he was divine, as we shall see in subsequent chapters; but they wished to retain the *son of David* tradition, and they felt the need to justify the claim by supplying a list of Jesus' ancestors, going back to David. The reader will sense that this is going to be a formidable commitment, but it was not beyond the wit of our first and third evangelists.

Matthew was writing in the late 70s, long after Mary's death (she would have been over 90). He knows hardly any *stories* about Jesus which did not come in Mark, but he constantly looks in Jesus' life for fulfilments of the Old Testament, which he knows in both Hebrew and Greek. It must have been a problem to many Christians how Jesus could have been Son of God; and Matthew found the answer in a prophecy of Isaiah, which read in the Greek:

> Behold, a virgin shall conceive and bear a son, and his name shall be called Emmanuel (Isa. 7.14).

Three features combined to assure Matthew that this was the answer: first his conviction that the history of salvation was foretold in prophecy; second, the promise of a *sign*, which often means *miracle*, that a *virgin* girl should conceive; and third the name Emmanuel, which means *God with us*. The Hebrew word *'alma* simply means a young woman, but the Greek word *parthenos* means a virgin girl, and it is this that makes the miracle, and so provides the answer – Jesus' father was God, and his mother Mary will have been a virgin at the time of his conception. Matthew is in a position to *infer* what *must have happened*, and he quotes the Isaiah verse, and the meaning of Emmanuel, to prove it (Matt. 1.18–25). Being rather a male chauvinist pig, he feels that God will have sent an angel to reassure Joseph; but no message to Mary herself will have been required.

What then about the son of David? Matthew starts with that: 'The book of the genealogy of Jesus Christ the son of David . . .' (1.1); and he provides a genealogy going back to Abraham – fourteen names from Abraham to David, fourteen from David to the exile, fourteen from the exile to Jesus. But the last step in the line is a shuffle: '. . . Jacob the father of Joseph *the husband of Mary, of whom Jesus was born, who is called Christ*' (1.16). So Jesus is not the *physical* son of David at all; he is *legally* son of Joseph, and so *adopted* son of David. Luke adopts exactly the same strategy: he gives seventy-seven ancestors of Jesus, right back to Adam, but the crucial link at the beginning is faulted – 'Jesus, when he began his ministry, was about

thirty years of age, being the son (*as was supposed*) of Joseph . . .'
(3.23). Physically, say both evangelists, he was God's Son, legally
Joseph's.

It is noticeable that Matthew and Luke supply very different lists
of ancestors. Matthew takes the line down from David through
Solomon and the line of kings of Judah; Luke takes it through
Nathan, Solomon's elder brother and supposedly the prophet. They
come together with Shealtiel and Zerubbabel, but again diverge,
Matthew with twelve, Luke with twenty-one names between Shealtiel
and Joseph. Luke's names often sound as if they come from the Old
Testament: Levi, Simeon, Judah, Joseph in succession, like the
patriarchs; Amos, Nahum, like the prophets; Eli, Matthat, Levi, like
the priests. In the third century people sometimes thought that the
names were symbolic, to indicate that Jesus was king, priest, prophet,
etc.; and one of the Fathers, Julius Africanus, writes a preposterous
reconstruction to prove they were wrong, and that Luke and Matthew
can be reconciled.

Matthew and Luke have provided a brilliant, and lasting, solution
to the two problems (How can Jesus have been the Son of God? How
can he at the same time have been the son of David?). We may notice
that neither of them takes the physical line back through Mary, since,
on their biological theory, this would not have worked; but Luke,
who is not an MCP, thinks that God would have had the courtesy to
inform Mary of what was happening. The weakness of their solution
is that it is not *orthodox*. Paulines believed, and in time the church
put into its creed, that Christ was an eternal being (God of
God . . .); but on their account he came into existence when the
Holy Spirit came upon Mary, in 1 BC. So if one looks too closely,
Matthew and Luke are heretics; but then, it has been decided not to
look too closely. St John saw the problem, and left their conception
stories out, but most Christians have felt they are too good to miss,
and do not notice the difficulty.

I mentioned scholars' suspicions that Peter did not really attach the
label *the Christ* to Jesus in his lifetime; William Wrede suggested this
in 1900, and the evidence seems to suggest that he was right. Wrede
pointed to the number of times in Mark where Jesus tells the disciples
to keep quiet. When Peter says, 'You are the Christ', Mark says, 'he

charged them to tell no one about him' (8.30). After the vision on the mount of Transfiguration 'he charged them to tell no one what they had seen, till the Son of Man should have risen from the dead' (9.9). Going through Galilee, Jesus 'would not have anyone know it; for he was teaching his disciples, saying to them, The Son of Man will be delivered . . .' (9.30f.).

These commands to silence come up a lot in other ways. Demons announce that Jesus is the Son of God 'and he strictly ordered them not to make him known' (3.12; cf. 1.25). A healed leper is told, 'See that you say nothing to anyone' (1.44). Jairus and his wife are 'strictly charged that no one should know' about the raising of their daughter (5.43). After the healing of the deaf and dumb man, 'he charged them to tell no one' (7.36). Even the parables are said to be told not to make the truth clear but to make it obscure: 'for those outside everything is in parables, so that they may indeed see but not perceive, and may indeed hear but not understand, lest they should turn again and be forgiven' (4.11f.).

William Wrede said that the picture Mark draws is incoherent and unbelievable. In many cases (the demons, Jairus' daughter, the deaf and dumb man) large numbers of people are present, so the command to silence is futile. In other cases (the Gerasene demoniac, Bartimaeus) no effort is made for silence, or proclamation is urged. Parables told to conceal the truth would be not merely cruel but pointless. So he suggested another reason for the secrecy motif.

Jesus preached the kingdom, and performed many healings and exorcisms; but there were other preachers of the kingdom like John Baptist, and other healers (Matt. 12.27). People would naturally use a general word for such holy men, like *prophet* (Luke 7.16). The thing that really made Jesus different was the resurrection experiences. After that his followers would be looking for a *unique* position for him, and *Christ* might then occur to Peter. But then how could a Christian preacher explain to his hearers that Jesus had never claimed such a title for himself – and the even higher title *Son of God*? So comes the explanation: *it was a secret*. The demons knew about it, and Jesus himself knew about it, and Peter divined it; but the thing was a secret, because Jesus was a Christ who had to suffer, a Son of God who must rise from the dead. The answer, Wrede said, was hinted at in Mark 9.9, 'he charged them to tell no one what they had seen, *till the Son of Man should have risen from the dead*'. You see, that was why no one had heard about Jesus' being Christ in his lifetime: they knew about it of course, but Jesus told them to keep quiet *till after the resurrection*.

15

The Possession Christology

The Messiah christology had a strong appeal in that it made Jesus the focus of many promises in the Old Testament: 'You are my Son', the shoot from the stump of Jesse, and so on. Luke speaks of this as the bottom line of Pauline preaching in the synagogues of Greece and Turkey: Apollos 'powerfully confuted the Jews in public, showing by the scriptures that *the Christ was Jesus*' (Acts 18.28; cf. 17.3). But in Palestine it was not so attractive. For one thing Jesus had not behaved at all like a king, and nobody in Galilee had seen him as a king; rather he had seemed to be like a prophet (Luke 17.16; John 7.40). Further, the idea of kingship smelt of insurrections, armies, fighting and war against Rome; and this was not at all what the Palestinian church intended, nor was it an impression it at all wished to give. Jesus had been put to death as 'the king of the Jews' (Mark 15.2,9,12,18,26), following the demonstration when he rode into Jerusalem (Mark 11.1–10); and a century later R. Aqiba would hail Bar-Kosiba as Messiah when he led the Second disastrous Jewish Revolt. So it is not surprising that the Palestinian churches preferred a different christology, more in line with Jesus' prophetic style of life.

Hitherto we have been able to offer evidence from the New Testament itself for the opinions of Petrines as well as Paulines: in loyalty and on practical issues, Matthew was a Petrine, and we have James and strands in Revelation, as well as fairly clear statements in Paul of what he is arguing against. But on the central doctrinal issues the Pauline churches which selected the New Testament were clear on what was orthodox and what was heresy, and they were not going to put into the Bible anything heretical. So Matthew was included because he was felt to be sound on christology (as well as being spiritually moving, and the church's greatest poet); and James has no apparent christology (he hardly mentions Jesus). Hence we are not going to find any straightforward statements of the Jerusalem christology in the New Testament itself, except where the Paulines agreed with it. We are therefore driven to go a rather longer way round.

When in church life there is an irreconcilable difference over important doctrine, there are winners and losers. The winning party becomes the church, and its opinion is orthodoxy (Greek *orthe doxa*, correct opinion); the losing party is driven out of the church and becomes a sect (Latin *secta*, a school under a particular teacher), or heresy (Greek *haeresis*, a party). In the early Christian church the Petrines won at Antioch (Gal. 2.11–14); but Paul played his cards carefully, and did not split away. In the second century the Paulines won, and the Aramaic churches split away (ch. 25) and became heretical sects, called the Ebionites and the Nazarenes. Their writings were all lost with time; but we have some traces of their teachings, partly in accounts given by orthodox Fathers (who may be more or less reliable), and partly in quotations, which may be assumed to be accurate. When we have clear, datable evidence from a later century, we can ask whether there is any reflection of such a view in the controversial documents in our New Testament. I shall argue that we have a statement of the Jerusalem christology in the account of the Ebionites given by Irenaeus, bishop of Lyons in France (180); that this is borne out by quotations from the Gospel of the Ebionites (150); that it is this position which is argued against by Ignatius (115) and in the letters and Gospel of John (100); that it is the basis of the gospel which was taken over and re-written by Mark (69), and is the teaching opposed by Paul (50–62).

Irenaeus was an active, careful, truthful man, whose influence was for the peace of the church (in line with his name – *eirene* means peace in Greek); and he wrote a large work in five books *Against the Heresies*. The dominant threat was from a development in Christianity called Gnosticism, and its two leading teachers Valentinus and Marcus. In Book I he devotes the first twenty-two chapters to these movements, and then in 1.23–31 he gives a brief account of the earlier (and surviving) groups which are tarred with the same brush. Only one of these shows clear signs of being Jewish Christian, the Ebionites, and this is what Irenaeus says about them:

Those who are called Ebionites agree [with the church] that the world was made by God; but their opinions with respect to the Lord are similar to those of Cerinthus (see below) and Carpocrates. They use the gospel according to Matthew only, and repudiate the Apostle Paul, maintaining that he was an apostate from the Law. As to the prophetical writings, they endeavour to expound them in a somewhat singular manner: they practise circumcision, persevere in those customs which are enjoined by the Law, and are so Judaic in their style of life that they even adore Jerusalem as if it were the house of God (*AH* 1.26.2).

The Ebionites are plainly Jewish Christians, and close to the positions which we have ascribed to the Jerusalem mission. They *circumcise*, observe *the Law* as prescribed by tradition (*those customs which are enjoined, are Judaic in their style of life*), and reverence *Jerusalem*. Their *somewhat singular* exposition of the prophets only means that they understood them differently from Irenaeus. As we should have expected for Jerusalem Christians, they *repudiated* the epistles of *Paul*, because he argues against observing the Law in its entirety; and they *used the Gospel of Matthew*, which is much the closest to a Jewish-Christian Gospel. We are not told that they used *all* the Gospel of Matthew, and they may well have dropped Matt. 1–2, as we shall see. If they used Matthew, they spoke Greek: the Aramaic speaking churches seem not to feature in Irenaeus' thinking. But the name Ebionites is Semitic: it is derived from the Hebrew word *'ebionim*, which means *poor*.

Irenaeus links the Ebionites' *opinions with respect to the Lord* to those of Cerinthus, which he sets out in the previous paragraph:

He represented Jesus as not having been born of a virgin, but as being the son of Joseph and Mary according to the normal course of human generation, while he nevertheless was more righteous, prudent and wise than other men. Moreover after his baptism, Christ descended into him in the form of a dove from the highest Ruler, and then he proclaimed the unknown Father, and performed miracles. But at last Christ departed from Jesus, and then Jesus suffered and rose again, while Christ remained

untouched by suffering, inasmuch as he was a spiritual being
(*AH* 1.26.1).

The Ebionites (and Cerinthus) thought Jesus was a straightforwardly
human being, just as is implied by Peter's Messiah, line-of-David
christology; and because the Paulines have by now come to believe
in the virginal conception, the contrast is set out clearly – he was
conceived *in the normal way by Joseph and Mary*. What was different
about Jesus was that he was especially good; and for a period, *from
his baptism to his crucifixion, he was possessed* by a heavenly spirit called
Christ. This spirit was sent not by God himself but by an archangel,
the highest Ruler, who is distinguished from *the unknown Father*. The
spirit is called Christ, quite a different use of the word from the
traditional one used in the Messiah approach. Jesus' possession by
this spirit enables him to do two things which he could not have done
naturally: he *proclaimed the unknown Father* – taught much about
God, referred to often as *your heavenly Father* in Matthew's Gospel
– and *performed miracles*. These two activities constituted the coming
of the kingdom of God, the core of the Petrine good news. But the
spirit, Christ, like any spiritual being, cannot suffer death, so it left
Jesus on the cross. So Jesus died on his own, and the cross is not a
significant part of the good news – just as in the teaching of the
Cephas Christians in I Cor. 1–2, which Paul contrasts with his gospel
of the cross. But the Ebionites did believe that *Jesus rose again* (in
some sense, see ch. 24); Paul says in I Cor. 15 that the resurrection
of Jesus was common ground between him and Peter and James.

Irenaeus' account of the Ebionites' christology is coherent and
rather persuasive. It reminds us of the occasions in the Old Testament
when the Spirit of the Lord comes upon certain heroes, enabling
them to perform superhuman deeds: Samson, so as to rend a lion,
or Elijah to run before King Ahab's chariot from Carmel to Jezreel.
Elijah and Elisha come particularly to mind because there are not
too many miracles in the Old Testament and Jesus' miracles do often
recall theirs (ch. 18). In their cases also we may speak of (more
temporary) *possession* by the Spirit.

For any further detail of Ebionite beliefs we are dependent upon
Epiphanius, bishop of Salamis in Cyprus nearly two centuries after

Irenaeus. Epiphanius was not greatly concerned for truth or charity, for heretics do not deserve such, and we have to treat his reports with care; but he does know some Ebionites, and he did have a copy of their Gospel, which he calls 'The Gospel of the Hebrews'. He wrote seventy books against the heretics, called the *Panarion*, which means the panacea; and the Ebionites are described in Book 30. I have already mentioned (p. 70) that they told him that their name arose from their forebears having shared their possessions, as it says in Acts 2–4, and so fallen into poverty. Epiphanius did not believe this, and supposed them to be cloaking the fact that the name came from their false teacher Ebion; so he has not made it up, and it is very likely true.

The most interesting things in Epiphanius come from his account of the Ebionite Gospel. He says that this work had no account of the Nativity and began with the Baptism of John (30.13.6). An early paragraph began:

When the people were baptized, Jesus also came and was baptized by John. And as he came up out of the water, the heavens were opened and he saw the Holy Spirit in the form of a dove that descended and entered into him. And a voice sounded from heaven that said, Thou art my beloved Son; in thee I am well pleased. And again, I have this day begotten thee (30.13.7).

There are three points here which confirm the picture which Irenaeus gave us. First, the absence of any story of Jesus' conception, birth or childhood is in line with a denial of the virginal conception, and a concentration on the baptism as the moment of divine initiative. Secondly, it is to be noticed that the Holy Spirit *descended and entered into Jesus*: such an expression is in line with a possession christology. Of our Gospels, Mark uses the similar phrase, *descending into him* (see ch. 18); but both Matthew and Luke carefully change this to *upon him*, and in John there is no baptism at all – the Baptist just *sees the Spirit descending and abiding on him*. Thus all the later Gospels seem to go out of their way to avoid the suggestion that Jesus was possessed at the Baptism. Two of them have just told us that Jesus was God's Son through the overshadowing of Mary, and John has said that he was the Word of God from eternity. Finally, the Ebionite

Gospel adds a sentence not found in any of our Gospels, *And again, I have this day begotten thee.* We have met this line from Ps. 2.7 in the last chapter, where it was applied to *the resurrection.* In the Messiah christology God *designated* Jesus his Son by the resurrection, and this text was used as proof of this in Acts 13.33 (and two or three times in Hebrews). But now it has been transferred to the Baptism, where it fits neatly after *Thou art my Son*, the first half of the verse in Ps. 2. So the *adoption*, as we may say, of Jesus as Son of God, happens for the Ebionites at the Baptism.

We may notice one or two further things about the Ebionite Gospel. There is one difference from Irenaeus' account. Although both held a possession view, with a human Jesus taken over by a divine spirit at the Baptism, they differ in the name of this spirit. According to Irenaeus it was a power called *Christ, sent by the highest Ruler*, while the Ebionite Gospel refers to it as *the Holy Spirit.* It is likely that *the Holy Spirit* was the earlier form of the teaching, because the Spirit of the Lord is the possessing power mentioned a number of times in the Old Testament, and this is where the idea is likely to come from. But there was much discussion of angelic powers in the first century (ch. 22), and giving of names to them; and if the possessing power was called Christ, it would be possible to marry together the possession and the Messiah christologies. Both taught a naturally conceived, fully human Jesus; both believed that his career as healer and preacher began with his baptism; both gave him the double name, Jesus/Christ. The naming of the possessing power as Christ solved the problem and saved the suggestion of anti-Roman rebellion.

For the end of the Ebionite Gospel we are without direct evidence. Its authors draw on all three of our Synoptic Gospels, but they prefer Matthew, and Matthew happens to give a rather ambiguous account of Jesus' death. He writes, 'And Jesus crying again with a loud voice let the spirit go' (Greek *apheken to pneuma*, 27.50). The modern reader takes this simply to mean *he breathed his last*; but a Jewish Christian reader would have no difficulty in understanding it as *he let the possessing Spirit, Christ, leave him* – particularly as Jesus has just said, *My God, my God, why have you forsaken me?* Ebionites might find this account of the death entirely satisfactory.

Irenaeus knew of the Ebionite Gospel, so it is generally allowed that it existed a generation before he was writing, say 150. Earlier than that we have little direct testimony, and shall have, in the next chapters, to make use of our powers of inference. Justin, who was martyred in Rome, wrote a famous *Dialogue with Trypho*, a learned Jew; and this may go back to the 130s. He speaks of certain (in his view semi-Christian) Jews who take Jesus to be Messiah, but as 'a man from men'; they deny the pre-existence of Jesus (i.e. the now orthodox Pauline-Johannine christology), and think he became Messiah by divine election (*Dial.* 48). This sounds very like the Ebionite view, with the 'election' taking place at the baptism. Otherwise the evidence of the Fathers is later than Irenaeus. Tertullian, around 200, says that 'Ebion' made Jesus *a mere man and only of the seed of David (De Carne Christi*, 14); and Epiphanius writes interestingly, 'The Ebionites say that the Spirit, which is Christ, came into him and clothed him who was called Jesus' (*Pan.* 30.16.3). Tertullian is closer to the Messiah christology, while Epiphanius uses the 'clothing' metaphor, which we find of the Spirit in Judg. 6.34; I Chron. 12.10; II Chron. 24.20.

This chapter has been an excursus into times beyond the New Testament. But it seems clear that, even where other views are later associated with Jewish Christians, a mainstream christology in their communities was the possessionist interpretation of Jesus. We find this in a Jewish Christian document, datable to around 150; it is the only christology associated by Irenaeus with Jewish Christians about 180; and it was one of the two or three enduring teachings among such communities, lasting at least two further centuries, till the time of Epiphanius. I shall suggest in the next chapters that we find a teaching of just this kind being opposed in New Testament documents around 100, in the Roman province of Asia; and indeed, that it goes back to the time of Paul.

16

The Possessionists in Asia

The Romans divided what we call Turkey into five provinces, of which the richest and most important was called Asia. It comprised most of the western coast of our Turkey and the well-watered hinterland; and it was here that the great battles were fought for the control of the Christian church. John's Gospel was written in Ephesus, its principal city, and the three Letters of John, around 100. A little earlier the Revelation of another John, the Seer, was composed for 'the seven churches in Asia'. A little later the Pastor wrote the two Letters to Timothy and one to Titus, with many references to Ephesus and Ephesian Christians. I Peter comes from about the same period (it was not written by St Peter), and is addressed to the five provinces. Ignatius wrote six of his seven letters to churches in the area about 115. Earlier Paul wrote Ephesians, Colossians and Philemon, three of his last letters, to Asian churches. The place was a hotbed of controversy (ch. 25).

Our fullest information comes from seven letters which were written by Ignatius, bishop of Antioch in Syria, while on his way to be martyred in Rome: he was escorted through Asia by a guard of ten soldiers, and he visited some of the churches in the province, and even attended church service. His journey was a rallying point for other churches besides, which sent deputations to see him before he was thrown to the lions. Ignatius made the most of his dramatic situation to press his own doctrinal views against the wrong-headedness of his opponents. The date usually given for his passage and death is around 117.

Ignatius was a Pauline. He writes to the Ephesians: 'You are associates in the mysteries with the blessed Paul, who obtained a good report, who is worthy of all felicitation; in whose footsteps I would be found treading, when I shall attain unto God; who in every letter makes mention of you in Christ Jesus' (*Eph.* 12). Ignatius is rather given to flattery, and it is not at all the case that Paul mentions the Ephesians in every letter, but there is no doubt of his being with the Paulines. Not only does he say so here, but he constantly inserts phrases from Paul's letters in his own, and compares himself, a little unctuously, to the apostle.

The central theme of Ignatius' letters is the threat from certain false teachers who deny the reality of the cross and resurrection: he often uses the word *really* – 'he really died, he was really raised' – the force of which I will discuss in a moment. His invariable solution to this problem is that the churches should unite round their bishop and presbytery: it is for this reason that Ignatius has been popular with clergy of the Church of England, and despised by the presbyterian Milton. From our point of view, this is simply another aspect of his Pauline sympathies. The bishop and the elders (presbyters) were the *local* ministry, that is the *Pauline leadership*. The false teachings have been propagated by *visiting missionaries*, so that they do not hold the power structure in the churches, even when they are a majority. It is the threat to the local leaders which has driven them to call on the passing martyr-to-be, so as to shore up their position.

Ignatius keeps on hammering at the central, christological issue. Only now and again does he mention other errors which the opposition are spreading. But in two of the letters it becomes clear that Jewish Christianity is a powerful force in Asia:

> For if even unto this day we live after the manner of Judaism, we avow that we have not received grace: for the divine prophets lived after Jesus Christ . . . If then those who had walked in ancient practices attained unto newness of hope, no longer observing sabbaths but fashioning their lives after the Lord's day, on which our life also arose through Him and through His death, which some men deny . . . how shall we be able to live apart from him? (*Magnesians*, 8f.).

There are Christians around who are *living after the manner of Judaism* and *observing sabbaths*; and they are perhaps also the *some* who *deny His death*. Ignatius argues, rather speciously, that the prophets were

persecuted by the Jews so they must have been *living after Jesus Christ*
and (in some surprising way) *fashioning their lives after the Lord's day*.
Anyhow sabbath-keeping and other Jewish ways are corrupting the
true pattern of Christian life.

In ch. 1 I quoted from Ignatius' letter to the Philadelphians:

> If anyone propound Judaism to you, do not listen to him . . . I
> cried out when I was among you; I spoke with a loud voice, with
> God's own voice, 'Give heed to the bishop and the presbytery and
> deacons' . . . I heard certain people saying, 'If I do not find it in
> the ancient texts, I do not believe it in the Gospel'; and when I
> said to them, 'It is written', they answered me, 'That is the
> question' (*Philadelphians* 6ff.).

Here again we have a Jewish Christian opposition in the church
(*propounding Judaism*). Ignatius tries the simple tactic of appealing to
the authority of the local church leaders, whom he knows will be
Paulines; and he supposes (or perhaps pretends) that his loud,
confident voice is a sign of divine inspiration. But the opposition are
not falling for that. He then tries appealing to 'the Gospel', very likely
John's Gospel which he has just cited, and which is an ultra-Pauline
document; and they refuse this too – they accept only the authority
of *the ancient texts*, i.e. the Old Testament. In other words they are
Jewish Christians throughout.

Magnesians and *Philadelphians* contain just the same central stress
of the *reality* of the cross and resurrection which we find in the other
letters. Here is the fullest statement of the issue:

> Be deaf therefore, when any man speaks to you apart from Jesus
> Christ, who was of the race of David, who was the son of Mary,
> who was truly born and ate and drank, was truly persecuted under
> Pontius Pilate, was truly crucified and died in the sight of those in
> heaven and those on earth and those under the earth; who
> moreover was truly raised from the dead . . . But if it were as
> certain persons say, that he suffered only in semblance, why am I
> in bonds? (*Trallians* 9f.).

These *certain persons* who *say that he suffered only in semblance* will be

the same as the *some* who *deny his death* in *Magn.* 8 above. But who is
the *he*? It has often been thought that it is *Jesus*, and the problem has
then been how anyone could be supposed to think that Jesus did not
really die; as if he was not really there on the cross and you could
have put your finger through what seemed to be his body. But a more
plausible suggestion is that they were speaking about *Christ*, with the
same christology as the Ebionites in the last chapter. This would be
much more convincing, for the Ebionites thought that Christ had
worked the miracles in Jesus, but had *remained without suffering
because he was a spiritual being*. Christ had left Jesus on the cross to
die alone: he had not suffered or risen again, it had only *looked as if*
Christ were suffering. When Paulines like Ignatius said, 'Jesus Christ
really suffered', they replied, 'Jesus suffered; it only *seemed* that
Christ suffered'.

The Greek word for *seemed* is *dokein*, and accordingly the opposition in Ignatius have usually been referred to as *Docetists*. This word
should be avoided because it encourages muddle, in particular the
unbelievable suggestion that the figure on the cross was a ghost.
The opposition were Jewish Christians, and they held the same
possessionist christology which we found in Cerinthus and the
Ebionites in Irenaeus. The same thing was going sixty years earlier.
Each time Ignatius mentions the *certain people (Magn.* 9; *Trall.* 10;
Smyrn. 2), it is the *suffering* and *death* which they say *seemed* to take
place; and it is precisely the suffering and death which are the point
at which the Ebionites make Christ leave Jesus. This would account
too for the other emphases in the passage. Jesus-Christ is a single
person, not a compound: Christ was not a heavenly being which
suddenly possessed Jesus at the baptism – he was one with Jesus in
a human ancestry going back to *David*, in being born of a human
mother *Mary*, in *eating and drinking*, and his crucifixion and death
are undeniable, having been witnessed in *heaven, earth and the
underworld*.

We may even have direct evidence that the opposition spoke of
Christ where Ignatius so constantly says *Jesus Christ* or *Christ Jesus*.
In *Ephesians* 14.2 he says, 'A tree is manifest from its fruit; so they
who profess to be *of Christ* will be seen through what they do'. The
opposition spoke of themselves as *of Christ*, a label which we shall
meet again in earlier writings: the key point of their belief was that

the divine power Christ entered the human Jesus, and through his miracles and revelations initiated the kingdom of God. Ignatius is a Pauline to whom the cross and resurrection were the cardinal points of religion. If the single eternal Jesus-Christ did not really suffer and rise from the dead, the whole thing collapses; Ignatius' martyrdom would then be pointless: *if he suffered only in semblance, why am I in bonds?*

Ignatius *was* thrown to the lions, and Polycarp, the bishop of Smyrna (Izmir) in Asia wrote to enquire of the Philippian church about it. In the letter he several times quotes our Letters to Timothy, so these are earlier than Ignatius – perhaps about the turn of the century. One feature which we may pick out at once that ties them to Ignatius is the regular, almost hyphenated, use of Jesus Christ or Christ Jesus where other New Testament documents are content with one name or the other. Jesus is referred to about 130 times in Ignatius, and of these 120 are in the form Jesus Christ or Christ Jesus. The Pastorals have Christ alone once only and the double name (in either order) 30 times. This at once suggests that both authors are facing the same threat, a christology which separates Christ from Jesus, and they are alike insisting on his unity by constantly combining the two names. There is no question that the opposition which the Pastorals are attacking are Jewish Christians: they are the circumcision party (Titus 1.10), teaching Jewish myths (1.14), and the Law, though they do not understand it (I Tim. 1.7).

The Pastorals are orthodox Pauline writings, as may be seen from their references to Jesus Christ's coming into the world, appearing, or being revealed in the flesh:

Christ Jesus came into the world to save sinners (I Tim. 1.15).

Great . . . is the mystery of our religion, he who was revealed in flesh (I Tim. 3.16).

The grace which he gave us in Christ Jesus ages ago, and now has manifested through the appearing of our Saviour Christ Jesus (II Tim. 1.9).

Jewish Christians thought that *Christ came into the world* at a different moment from Jesus; they denied that Christ *was revealed in the flesh* at all, and that *Christ Jesus has* been *manifested*, or has *appeared* as a single being. Although these statements might not be polemical, there are others which are. The reference in Titus 1.14, 'not attending to Jewish myths and commandments of men who turn aside the truth' is plainly against Jewish Christians. We have spoken before of the *commandments of men*, the interpretations of the Law by Jewish sages (ch. 4); the *Jewish myths* are accounts of proceedings in heaven with angels and other powers supposedly in action. Something of this kind underlies the Ebionite view, where the heavenly Christ was sent by the Supreme Ruler (who is not *the Unknown Father*); and we have more developed forms in the Gnostic myths. The Pastorals are defending Pauline incarnational christology against Jewish Christian myths justifying possessionism.

An example of a polemical statement is probably I Tim. 2.5: 'there is one mediator between God and men, the man Christ Jesus'. Someone is maintaining something different, or the emphasis would not be necessary. Well, we know from Ignatius that there were people holding Jewish Christian views, who thought that the mediator between God and men was the *angelic power* Christ, not *the man Christ Jesus* at all; and while we cannot be sure that this was the doctrine under attack, it fits well.

More famously there is a kind of brief creed at I Tim. 3.16, which should probably be read in the same way:

> Great, we confess, is the mystery of our religion:
> He who was manifested in flesh,
> Vindicated in spirit,
>   Appeared to angels;
> Preached among Gentiles,
> Believed on in the world,
>   Taken up in glory.

The verse is difficult, and with difficult verses the best method is to begin with the easiest part. It looks as if lines 5 and 6 belong together, and are a hit against narrow-minded Petrine people who thought that the kingdom was really for Jews: no, says the Pastor, Christ Jesus *was preached among Gentiles* and in fact *was believed in in the world*, which is more than can be said for the response of the Jewish people. Lines 2 and 3 similarly belong together, and would also be written to oppose Petrine teaching. The Jewish Christian (Ebionite) movement denied vigorously that *Christ Jesus was revealed in flesh*: they thought that Jesus was a man of flesh like us, and Christ possessed him. But of course all through the Bible there is a contrast between *flesh* and *spirit*. Paulines believed that God vindicated Jesus Christ by raising him from death: *he was vindicated* by God *in spirit*, as in Rom. 1.4, 'designated Son of God in power according to the Spirit of holiness by his resurrection'. Petrines maintained that Christ was an angelic spirit, but the Pastor denies this: *he appeared to angels*, but that was as far as angels came into it: we had the angels as witnesses of the crucifixion mentioned above in *Trallians* 10. Finally the [resurrection and] ascension close the story. The Petrines had Christ leave Jesus on the cross, and Jesus resurrected independently; as a mere man he had no share in the divine glory. But for the Paulines Christ Jesus was a single eternal being, on an equality with God: *he was taken up in glory* without any question.

Both Ignatius and the Pastorals have offered problems to scholars: and the problem usually takes the form, 'Who are the opposition?' No one can claim to provide a final answer to such a long debated difficulty. What we can say is that (1) there is plenty of evidence that Jewish Christians are at least part of the opposition in both cases; and (2) that everything that is said about Jesus Christ fits the controversy we have found with the Ebionites, and which we shall trace yet earlier in the next two chapters.

17

John and the Possessionists

There are strong and bitter feelings in Ignatius and the Pastorals about the false beliefs of their opponents: but the feelings behind John's First Letter are extremely strong and bitter:

> Beloved, do not believe every spirit, but test the spirits to see whether they are of God; for many false prophets have gone out into the world. By this you know the Spirit of God: every spirit which confesses that Jesus Christ has come in the flesh is of God, and every spirit which does not confess Jesus is not of God. This is the spirit of antichrist, of which you heard that it was coming, and now it is in the world already.

The context in which the tension arises is (like that over the arrival of the kingdom in II Thess. 2) the church meeting. At such meetings Christians were liable to have 'revelations' (I Cor. 14.30), when a *spirit*, or angel, was understood to have communicated some import-ant truth to a church member. These revelations might be genuine spiritual insights; but often they were a means of manipulating the community, as we saw over the visions in Col. 2.16–18. The Paulines were in difficulties over such claims. They could not deny them absolutely because they sometimes claimed them themselves. But they knew that they were a menace in the hands of unscrupulous Petrines, and they tried to work out some criterion by which they could tell the genuine from the bogus, to *test the spirits to see whether they are of God*.

The Pauline ministry was locally based (ch. 11), but the Jerusalem mission had to depend on volunteers who were sent out in pairs from Palestine to go round the churches in other provinces and bring them into line. These are the visiting prophets mentioned in the *Didache* (ch. 11), and John speaks of them as *many false prophets who have gone out into the world*. Before 70 they had gone out from Jerusalem; after the Jewish War it will have been from other centres, perhaps Pella across the Jordan, to which Eusebius says the Jerusalem Christians fled (*Ecclesiastical History*, 3.5.3). John can tell they are *false* by a doctrinal criterion. *Every spirit which confesses that Jesus Christ has come in the flesh is of God* – that is everyone who (in trance, vision, etc.) agrees with John. John believed that Jesus-Christ was an eternal divine being, *the Word*, who had *come in the flesh*, i.e. had been incarnated for thirty-three years, or however many. But there were other spirits *which did not confess Jesus*, and they were *false*. *Confessing* is a technical religious word which means to ascribe divinity to, to worship. The trouble with the false prophets is that they *do not confess Jesus*. They confess Christ all right, but not Jesus. This is exactly the position which was maintained by the Ebionites, the Jerusalem Christians of ch. 15. They thought that Jesus was totally human, but that Christ was the name of the power which possessed him from the baptism to the cross: so they *confessed* Christ but *not Jesus*.

In John's church there is war to the knife. Some members have already set up a separate church: 'they went out from us but they were not of us' (I John 2.19). The visiting prophets are 'those who would deceive you' (2.26), and John sees them as diabolical. We saw in ch. 12 the Pauline interpretation of the evil king in Dan. 11 as 'the man of sin', and John calls him 'the antichrist'. I John 4.3 speaks of him as an active spirit now at work in these Petrine emissaries, and he says much the same in 2.22:

> Who is the liar but he who denies that Jesus is the Christ? This is the antichrist, he who denies the Father and the Son.

The *liars* do not deny that Jesus is the Christ in the old Petrine sense, that he is the awaited king of the line of David; the stress is on the word *is*. They *do not confess Jesus*, and think that Christ entered Jesus at the baptism; they deny that Jesus *is* Christ, that Jesus-Christ is a single, eternal being. In so saying, they in effect *deny the Son*, because they reduce Jesus from a divine being, *the Son*, to a merely human being; and if Jesus is not the Son, then God is not the Father, so *they deny the Father* as well. This was, to John, pretty clearly the work of antichrist.

He returns to Jesus' being the Son of God at 5.5:

This is he who came by water and blood, Jesus Christ, not in the water only but in the water and the blood. And the Spirit is the witness, because the Spirit is the truth. There are three witnesses, the Spirit, the water and the blood; and these three are united (Greek *eis to hen eisin*, 5.6ff.).

Jesus Christ is a single being to John, almost always spoken of as Jesus Christ or Christ Jesus, exactly as in Ignatius and the Pastorals. On one Jewish biological theory people are compounds of two basic elements, blood and water, and their characters are determined by whether these elements are properly balanced (*Leviticus Rabba*, 15): so *he came by* (Greek *dia*) *water and blood* means that the heavenly being Jesus-Christ came into the world in normal human form, a balance of blood and water. *He did not come in* (Greek *en*) *the water only*, as the Ebionite opposition say, viz. in the baptism where Christ is supposed to have entered and possessed Jesus; *but in the water and in the blood* of common humanity at his birth. This fundamental truth was *witnessed to* by *the Spirit* which spoke in Jesus to this effect (often, in John's Gospel). There are in fact *three who bear witness, Spirit, water and blood, and these three are united* in the one human-divine being Jesus-Christ, not divided, as the opposition say, into a human being, Jesus, of blood and water, and a divine Spirit which possessed him.

John has put the same teaching in graphic and memorable form in the Gospel, as Jesus dies. In Matthew Jesus had 'let the spirit go', and wrong-headed people could take this to mean that the possessing Spirit had left him. John will not have that, and he writes, 'and bowing his head he handed over the spirit' (John 19.30). Many translations have 'he gave up', but the Greek word is *paredoken, he handed over*. John wishes to emphasize Jesus' control throughout – the spirit did not leave him, he handed it over to God. The soldiers then come to make sure he is dead before Joseph may bury him; one of them drives a lance into his chest, *and at once there came out blood and water*. You see, says John, he was one divine-human being: *there*

*are three that bear witness, the Spirit and the water and the blood; and
these three are united in one.*

In the First Letter John speaks in general terms of the opposition,
but in the Gospel he makes it clear who they are:

> Jesus then said to the Jews who had believed in him, If you
> continue in my word, you are truly my disciples, and you will know
> the truth, and the truth will make you free. They answered him,
> We are descendants of Abraham, and have never been in bondage
> to anyone. How is it that you say, You will be made free? Jesus
> answered them, . . . I speak of what I have seen with my Father,
> and you do what you have heard from your father . . . Truly, truly,
> I say to you, before Abraham was, I am. So they took up stones to
> throw at him; but Jesus hid himself, and went out of the temple
> (John 8.31–59).

The (to us surprising) fact is that this blistering dialogue is not with
the Jews, who are so often the opposition in John, but with *the Jews
who had believed in him*, that is the Jewish *Christians*. The opening
verses recall Paul's altercations with Jewish Christians (Petrines) in
Gal. 4 and II Cor. 11. There also Paul sees salvation as resting in
faith in Jesus and obedience to his command to love, whereas the
Petrines' confidence lies in their being the *descendants of Abraham*,
circumcised Jews. To Paul and John the Law is *bondage* while
Christian discipleship is *freedom*. But behind the issue of the Law
and circumcision there is the bigger christological question. For the
Paulines, Jesus Christ is an eternal being: *I speak of what I have seen
with my Father* (8.38), *before Abraham was, I am* (8.58). For the Jewish
Christians this is blasphemy, since God is one, and the Paulines put
Jesus on a parity with God – *the Son* with *the Father*, the claim that
my word replaces the Law and offers *freedom* in place of bondage, the
I am which recalls the name of God in Ex. 3.14, *I am that I am*. The
penalty for blasphemy was stoning, and *they took up stones to throw at
him*. So Petrines regard Paulines as blasphemers. But just as in
I John Paulines speak of Petrines as being *of the antichrist* , so now
they *have heard* their teaching *from their father*; and in 8.44, the
camouflage net comes off the gun, *You are of your father the devil*.
There is no hatred like the hatred of brothers in faith.

We have a similar altercation in John 6, where Jesus has been speaking of himself as 'the living bread which came down from heaven'. In 6.41 the Jews murmur at him for this, and at 6.52 they dispute among themselves how this may be. Jesus then speaks of the necessity of eating his flesh and drinking his blood for eternal life: one must, in other words, receive the sacrament of the eucharist, and one must accept the incarnation doctrine, that Jesus Christ is an eternal being who *came down from heaven*. The sacramental bread is *the Word made flesh*, an extension of Jesus Christ's life in the flesh. But at 6.60 we read, 'Many of his disciples, when they heard it, said, This is a hard saying; who can hear it?' and at 6.66, 'After this many of his disciples drew back and no longer walked with him'.

John is telling a story on two levels, as in John 8 above. Whatever memories survive of discussions in Jesus' lifetime, the evangelist's interest is in the situation of his own day. Christianity did not become a religion independent of Judaism on the day of Pentecost. Jewish Christians saw themselves as Jews still, but Jews with the key belief that Jesus was the Christ of the line of David, or the prophet possessed by the Spirit who proclaimed the arrival of the kingdom. The only Christians who did not think of themselves as Jews were the Pauline Gentiles: to them Judaism with its Law and circumcision and so on was an alien tradition. To them the new patch could not be sewn on to the old garment, nor the new wine go into the old bottles. The church was something new. So they saw the Jewish Christians as still being part of *Judaism*. They were *Jews disputing among themselves*; they were *disciples*, but disciples of whom the incarnation/eucharistic doctrine was *a hard saying which they could not hear*; they were *disciples who drew back and no longer walked with Jesus*. John is careful not to include Peter among these. He needs to have a tradition for his church which goes back to the first disciples, so Peter has to be on the side of the angels; and in fact the real christological battles did not develop until the 60s (with Colossians and Philippians) when Peter was probably dead. So although it is convenient for us to speak of the Jerusalem Christians as Petrines, we should strictly speaking remember that after his death both sides claimed Peter as having been for them.

The christological question did not come up for years because there were more urgent matters at stake, the practical matters which I have outlined, keeping sabbath and food and other purity laws, circumcision and sexual ascesis and differences over money and work. Then when it became clear that Paul was running a semi-independent mission with success, came the problem of whether he counted as an apostle or not. These were issues affecting everyday life, and it is these which fill the canvas of all but the later Pauline letters. Nevertheless we find hints that there is a christological divide as early as the Corinthian letters in the mid-50s. I mention two passages briefly here, and return to Colossians and Philippians in ch. 22.

In II Cor. 10–12 Paul is answering a series of attacks that have been made on him; and among his responses he says:

I feel a divine jealousy for you, for I betrothed you to Christ, to present you as a pure bride to her one husband. But I am afraid that as the serpent deceived Eve by his cunning, your thoughts will be led astray from a single-minded devotion to Christ. For if the visitor preaches another Jesus than the one we preached, or if you receive a different spirit from the one you received, or if you accept a different gospel from the one you accepted, you submit to it readily enough (II Cor. 11.2–4).

Again we have the *visiting* missionary (Greek *ho erchomenos*, the comer) from Jerusalem ('Are they Hebrews?', 11. 22), with a *different gospel*. The gospel might be different in that it was all about keeping the Law, and *the spirit* might be *different* in that it was all about tongues and visions; but there is also the *preaching of another Jesus*. It is not a different Christ; Paul and the visitor seem to be agreed on the divinity of Christ – it is Jesus over whom the preaching differs. In 11. 2 Paul stressed that he had intended the Corinthian church to be the bride of *one husband*, and the *jealousy* of which he speaks is the divine jealousy that Israel should be faithful to its *one God*: Paul fears they may fall from their *single-minded devotion* (Greek *haplotetos*) *to Christ*. So the suspicion rises that even here we have a Petrine *gospel* with a different, human *Jesus*, who is not *one* being with the heavenly Christ.

This seems to be confirmed by a passage in the first Corinthian Letter:

Now concerning spiritual gifts, brethren, I do not want you to be ignorant. You know that when you were heathen, you were led astray to dumb idols, however you may have been moved. Therefore I want you to understand that no one speaking by the Spirit of God ever says, Jesus be cursed!, and no one can say, Jesus is Lord, except by the Holy Spirit (I Cor. 12.1–3).

The Corinthians have written to ask Paul a series of questions, and he answers each point beginning, *Now concerning* . . . Here they have written to enquire about *spiritual gifts*: the question is, Is it really the Spirit of God speaking when someone cries out under 'inspiration', Damn Jesus? The situation is not difficult to imagine. The church is divided (as we have seen) into those of Paul and those of Cephas, who are mentioned alongside a group 'those of Christ' (1.12). The Paulines believe Jesus to be divine, and cry out in the worship, 'Jesus is Lord!'; and this exasperates the Petrines, who think Jesus to be a mere human being. After all Peter had *known* him, and James was his *brother*, so they ought to know. Wild assertions giving Jesus the name of God ('Lord') were blasphemous, so an angry Petrine feels inspired to shout out *Anathema Iesous*, Damn Jesus! Now, says the wise apostle, *you know* how easily you are *led astray*; it is only yesterday that you were worshipping *dumb idols*! Of course you are not used to the Holy Spirit which speaks. But the principle is quite simple: if the words are blasphemous, it cannot be *the Holy Spirit*; and if anyone says 'Jesus is Lord', that will be *the Holy Spirit*. Paul felt quite confident that the Holy Spirit was Pauline.

The context, and the issue, are extraordinarily close to John 4.1–3, from which we began. In both passages we have a scene of worship at a church meeting, with ecstatic crying (*spiritual gifts, spirits, prophets*). In both cases the community is divided on christological doctrine. Paul and John believe in the incarnation (*Jesus is Lord, Jesus Christ has come in the flesh*), and their opponents devalue Jesus (*Jesus be cursed, every spirit that does not confess Jesus*). In both cases a doctrinal (Pauline) criterion is provided for *testing the spirits*. So it looks as if the possessionist christology, with a divine Christ taking over the human Jesus, goes back to the 50s. Perhaps we have an explanation for the 'of Christ' group too: they were just Petrines stressing that they believed in Christ, but not in Jesus.

18

Possessionists before Mark

I Cor. 12 seems to give us a hint that there were Christians in Corinth in the 50s who took the Ebionite line. But have we any indication that the possession view was more widely held, and that it came from Jerusalem? Indeed we have.

Mark is our earliest Gospel, written about 69, and twice Mark mentions some *wrong* answers to the question Who was Jesus? At 8.28 we are told people said he was John Baptist, or Elijah, or one of the prophets; and the same three suggestions come at 6.14f. King Herod said, 'John the baptizer has been raised from the dead; that is why these powers are at work in him'. Now Mark will hardly have been concerned to tell his congregation wild ideas people had forty years before. It is much more likely that he gives the wrong ideas *because they are current in his own time*; especially when he gives them twice. There were Christians around in the 60s who thought these things.

The *John Baptist* theory is the most puzzling; after all Jesus and John were contemporaries, and John had baptized Jesus, so how could Jesus be thought to be John risen again? Perhaps we have a hint from the *Elijah* theory. In the Old Testament Elijah was taken up to heaven, and his mantle fell on his disciple Elisha, with a 'double portion of his spirit', so that Elisha was able to do twice as many miracles as his master. Herod's comment, *that is why these powers are at work in him*, suggests something similar. John Baptist was thought by some Christians to have been Elijah come down from heaven (Mark 9.13; Matt. 17.12f.; 11.14); and Jesus would then be carrying on his work, but with far more miracles. Elijah and Elisha are in fact, apart from Moses, the great miracle-workers in the Old Testament. They were ordinary human beings, prophets, and the Spirit of the

Lord, or the hand of the Lord, was liable to fall on them and enable them to do these marvels. This sounds very close to the Ebionite doctrine that the angelic Christ possessed the human Jesus from his baptism to his passion.

I have tried to show throughout this book that Mark was a Pauline, and he thought that any possession theory on the lines of Elijah or a prophet was a mistake. But Mark was not the first Christian to present an overall picture of the gospel. No believer just knew a few stories about Jesus. Everyone in the church had some idea of how the whole story fitted together, and Mark will have taken over the gospel outline that was in circulation before him, and adapted it. If the picture is correct which I suggested on p. 20, then Mark will have heard the stories told by Peter and the others in his mother's home in Jerusalem (Acts 12.12), and begun with their view of the gospel outline. We have always to remember that the only disciples who feature in the incidents in Mark are Peter, James and John, the three Jerusalem leaders in early days.

What is so striking is the similarity between the Marcan outline and the Ebionite outline. The Ebionites had no birth stories, and nor has Mark. They start the Gospel with John's preaching and his baptizing Jesus, and so does Mark. They believed that the angelic power entered Jesus at his baptism and enabled him to work miracles, and so does Mark. The miracle stories Mark tells are often reminiscent of the Elijah-Elisha miracles. The Ebionites thought that Christ left Jesus on the cross: Mark does *not* think that, but he does retain a saying which seems to imply it – according to him Jesus' words just before he died were, 'My God, my God, why did you forsake me?' So it looks as if we can descry behind our present *Pauline* Gospel of Mark a *pre-Pauline, Jerusalem* Gospel outline. Just as later Matthew was to re-write Mark to make it more Petrine, so Mark took over the earlier version of the Gospel (whether written or oral) and made it more Pauline, with stories of how Jesus had stood out against the sabbath- and food-laws, and so on.

Mark begins with a quotation from the Old Testament about John Baptist: 'Behold, I send my messenger before thy face . . .' This comes from Malachi (3.1), and it turns out in Mal. 4.5 that this messenger is Elijah the prophet. Indeed, Elijah 'wore a garment of haircloth, with a girdle of leather about his loins' when he went up to heaven (II Kings 1.8), and this is what John is wearing in Mark 1.6. Just as Elisha asked Elijah for the gift of his spirit (an elder son's portion, that is a double portion) at the Jordan, so does John baptize Jesus in the Jordan, and he receives the Holy Spirit. Mark says 'he saw the heavens opening and the Spirit descending *into* him like a dove' (1.10). This is the possessionist *into*: Matthew and Luke both carefully change it to *upon*, and John leaves the baptism out altogether. Mark does not believe the possessionist christology, but he has left the *into* in by oversight. The Jerusalem church quoted Isaiah 42.1 to explain what happened at the baptism: 'Behold, my servant whom I have chosen, my beloved with whom my soul is well pleased. I will put my Spirit on him . . .' (Matt. 12.18). Mark changed *my servant* to *my Son* to fit in better with Pauline ideas.

Elijah twice went into the desert. In I Kings 17 he flees, and he is fed by ravens. In I Kings 19 he flees again, and an angel provides him with a cake and a jar of water; and he goes in the strength of this food for forty days. After his baptism Jesus goes into the desert for forty days; he was with the wild animals, who seem to have been his companions; and angels ministered to him (Mark 1.12–13). Mark has added that Satan tempted him, but he does not tell us anything about the temptations.

Elijah received his commission in I Kings 19, and he returns and begins his ministry by calling a disciple, Elisha. The latter is ploughing, and asks to go and kiss his father farewell; but God's summons has to be obeyed at once, and he responds, burning his plough and sacrificing his animals on the fire. Jesus returns from the desert to begin his preaching. He calls his first disciples, Peter and Andrew, James and John, from their trade as they are fishing, and they at once respond to the call, leave all and follow him (Mark 1.14–20). Later in the Gospel tradition, Jesus will call a man who asks first to be allowed to go and bury his father; Jesus says, 'Leave the dead to bury the dead' – anyone who *puts his hand to the plough* and looks back is unworthy of the kingdom (Luke 9.60ff.).

In Mark 1.21–28 Jesus casts out a demon from a man in the synagogue, and the possessed man cries out, 'What have we to do with you, Jesus of Nazareth? I know you who you are, the holy one of God'. Those who know Mark's Gospel may find this disappointing. The demons live in the heavenly world, and they know the heavenly secrets: later on demons will cry out, 'You are the Son of God!' (3.11; 5.7), and Mark and his readers believe that Jesus is the Son of God. But here the demon just calls Jesus 'the holy one of God', God's saint. That was the title given to David in Ps. 16.10, 'Thou dost not give me up to Hades, Nor suffer *thy holy one* to see corruption'; the verse is quoted in Peter's sermon in Acts 2.31, and the title is used by Peter at Acts 3.14 and John 6.69. So it is likely that Jerusalem Christians told the story with their title for Jesus, the holy one of God, while Mark altered the later, similar stories to accommodate the Pauline title, the *Son* of God.

At Mark 1.40–45 Jesus cleanses a leper, as Elisha cleansed the leper Naaman in II Kings 5. Later Jesus raises a dead child to life, the twelve-year-old daughter of Jairus, as Elijah raised the dead son of the woman of Zarephath (I Kings 17), and Elisha raised the dead son of the woman at Shunem (II Kings 4). In Luke 7 Jesus raises the dead son of the widow at Nain, a story even closer to the Old Testament original. In Mark 6 Jesus feeds a crowd of 5,000 with five loaves; at first when he says, 'Give them to eat', his disciples hesitate, but he commands, and the crowd is fed, and twelve baskets of crumbs are left over. In II Kings 4.42–44 Elisha tells his servant to feed a crowd of a hundred from twenty loaves; the man hesitates, but the prophet insists, and there is bread left over. It is difficult to escape the feeling that these Elijah-Elisha stories have had an influence on the traditions about Jesus.

Also in Mark 6 John Baptist is executed. King Herod does not want to kill him, but he is weak, and under the influence of his wicked wife Herodias, who schemes against John, he gives her daughter John's head on a charger. In I Kings 19 King Ahab was unwilling to kill Elijah, but his wicked wife Jezebel was willing, and her threats forced Elijah to flee. Mark says that Elijah has come in John Baptist, 'and they did to him all they wanted, as it has been written of him' (Mark 9.13). Weak king and hard queen got him in the end.

The old Jerusalem gospel did not see John Baptist as a mere forerunner and Jesus as the Divine Son of God. They saw Jesus as John's successor when John was arrested (Mark 1.14), and the two as like Elijah and Elisha, his successor, in days of old. Some of John's disciples became Jesus' followers (John 1.35–40), and the Christian movement took over the basic message, 'Repent, for the kingdom is at hand' (Matt. 3.2, John; 4.17, Jesus), and the basic symbol, baptism in water, as the means of admission to the kingdom. Malachi had prophesied that Elijah would come to warn of Judgment Day, and John was understood to be Elijah returned. When he was executed, and Judgment Day did not come, Jesus was seen as a new Elisha. It was the Pauline movement which elevated Jesus to divine status and depressed John. Sometimes in Matthew, always the most Jewish-Christian Gospel, John and Jesus seem to be equals (11.16–19). In Mark he is still Elijah, but just as forerunner to Jesus, the Son of God. By John's Gospel he is Elijah no more (1.21), nor the prophet; he is just a voice crying in the wilderness (1.23).

The denial that John was 'the prophet' is significant too. In Deut. 18.15 it was promised that God would raise up a prophet like Moses from among their brethren, and it is added 'Him you shall heed'. In Mark 9 the disciples go up the mountain with Jesus (rather as the elders went up Sinai with Moses, or Elisha with his servant in II Kings 6). They see Jesus speaking with Moses and Elijah, and God's voice says from the cloud of glory, 'This is my beloved Son: *heed him*, (9.7). Up to Mark 9 Jesus has been very like Elijah and Elisha, especially in his miracles. After Mark 9 Jesus seems more to be the prophet like Moses. He upbraids the faithless generation that will not trust him (9.19), like Moses in Deut. 32.5. He overrides Moses' ruling on divorce in favour of the principle in Genesis (Deut. 24.1–4; Mark 10.1–12). He adds an extra principle to Moses' Ten Commandments (Deut. 5.16–20), to give away all that we have (Mark 10.17–31). He discounts the argument from Deut. 25.5 that remarriage of a dead brother's wife sheds doubt on the resurrection (Mark 12.18–27), and proclaims the love commandment of Lev. 19.18 to be the first of all. So the Jesus whom the Jerusalem mission honoured was the prophet like Moses promised by Deut. 18.15 and a new Elisha following the returned Elijah of Malachi; the divine Spirit had entered him at baptism, and produced these marvellous teachings and miracles.

The cross was an embarrassment to the Jerusalem Christians. They knew the Spirit could not die, and must therefore have left Jesus before his death; and here a quotation from the Psalms suggested itself. Psalm 22 opened, 'My God, my God, why did you forsake me?' and there are passages in Jewish writing where the word

'*Elohim* (God) is used for a divine spirit other than God himself. Even in I Sam. 28.13 the witch of Endor cries out as she sees Samuel's ghost, 'I see a god coming up out of the earth'. In the Dead Sea Scrolls the word is used of the angel Melchizedek (11Q Melch.); and in the apocryphal Gospel of Peter Jesus cries as he dies, 'My power, O power, you have forsaken me!' – Jesus' divine power has left him, and is spoken of in a psalm-verse which used '*Elohim*. Matthew also makes this verse Jesus' dying cry (but in Hebrew), and says, 'And Jesus, crying again with a loud voice, let the Spirit go' (27.50) Perhaps such a sentence closed the Jerusalem gospel: Jesus let the (angelic) Spirit go.

Preachers find this tradition of Jesus' last words a problem, especially on Good Friday, when the tradition is to preach on the Words from the Cross. What are they to say? I sat at lunch one day listening to a Catholic priest and an Anglican deacon discussing the question. The priest said that Jesus knew the whole of Ps. 22 by heart, and he did not think just of v. 1: from v. 22 the tone of the psalm turns to God's praise – 'I will tell of thy name to my brethren . . .' – and Jesus was simply citing a psalm which closely described his sufferings, but rested ultimately in confidence in God. The deacon asked if Mark's congregation was expected to know Ps. 22 by heart; otherwise, she said, would they not get the impression that Jesus had *lost* his faith, and would Mark not be obliged to indicate the later note of faith? This was certainly the condition of her congregation.

The priest obviously felt that she had scored a point which had been missed at the Gregorian University, and asked what she made of it. It was, she said, a part of the cost of incarnation. Crucifixion would mean not just physical agony for anyone, but also the sense of desolation, of being deserted by God; and it meant the same for Jesus. This left the priest surprised and dubious; and I sympathized with him. Perhaps she was right about the incarnation; but surely Mark would not want to leave his people with the impression that Jesus had lost his faith, and that God had let him down? Mark expected some of his congregation to have to face persecution and death, and the united message of the Bible is that God is faithful, and that his saints may depend on him. The incarnation approach was a bit too modern for Mark.

'My God, my God . . .' is in fact there because it was a firm part of Christian tradition, taught by Jewish Christians for decades to explain how the divine Spirit left the human Jesus. Mark makes a bit of a joke of it by saying that the soldiers thought he was calling on Elijah; but the Paulines were uncomfortable with it. Luke cuts it out and replaces it with another psalm-verse which is a bit more edifying, 'Father, into thy hands I commend my spirit'. John leaves it out too, and makes Jesus' final word a cry of triumph, 'It is finished!' The Pauline preachers were not happy with the old Jerusalem christology, and they dropped it; and my advice to a modern orthodox preacher is to do the same.

So the 'Ebionite' christology, which we found first described in Irenaeus about 180 is not the invention of the late second century. It was the creed of the Jerusalem church from early times. It underlies the earliest Pauline Gospel, Mark, and is evidenced from the middle 50s in Paul's first letter to Corinth, where people sometimes cursed Jesus in church. Peter's original Messiah christology raised difficulties which I have mentioned, and the mother-church adopted the simple Old Testament picture. The Spirit had possessed Elijah and Elisha (and Moses before them), and now he was at work again in John (who was Elijah returned) and Jesus his successor. The two teachings were married together by speaking of the possessing Spirit as the angelic power Christ: 'Christ' had entered Jesus at baptism, and left him on the cross.

The Paulines became the church, and in time they called the Jerusalem mission Ebionites, and made them a heresy. But heresies do not die easily, and today it is the orthodox incarnation doctrine which finds itself under pressure. How singular that our generation should have brought back a doctrine similar to (though not identical with) possessionism! For this is roughly the position of the Spirit christology advocated by Geoffrey Lampe, and earlier by Donald Baillie. It comes in the writings of John Hick and Maurice Wiles, and achieved a brief *succés de scandale* in a symposium to which I myself contributed, *The Myth of God Incarnate*.[1]

[1]John Hick (ed.), *The Myth of God Incarnate*, SCM Press 1977, second edition 1993.

19

The Need for Incarnation

Jewish people were not afraid that they would be sent to hell. Many of them did think that there was an 'age to come', a 'life to come'; but they could look forward to this. They were God's people, and he had promised that he would be their God. He had given them the Law and they had (roughly) kept it; and when they had not, they had repented (a bit), and God had undertaken to forgive Israel's sins each year at the Day of Atonement. Perhaps arch-hypocrites like Dives in the parable might be in trouble; but ordinary Israelites had nothing to fear. So baptism did not bring them *salvation* if they became Christians; they were saved already. It made them *spiritual, perfect*; members of the kingdom of God.

Gentile people were less fortunate. When Jews were persecuted by Gentiles they imagined that God would wreak vengeance on their tormentors after death; and as Gentiles were *not* God's people and did *not* keep his Law, it was natural to think that they would all go to Gehenna (hell). Many Gentiles too, on their own, thought of eternal tortures for the wicked, and Virgil pictures them suffering in Tartarus. So there was widespread anxiety, especially among any associated with the synagogue. When they died they would have to stand judgment before God, and they very much wanted to be acquitted, declared innocent, on that Day, not condemned to eternal torment or destruction. So baptism meant something different for Paul's Gentile converts than it did for the Jewish church-members: it was their means of salvation, their entry into God's people. Jewish Christians had joined God's people by circumcision, if they were men.

So Paul and other missionaries to the Gentiles faced a problem: how could Jesus' life have any effect on a Gentile? Why should being baptized bring him acquittal on the Day of Judgment? Paul thought about this a lot, and he came up with a number of different answers. All his solutions take the cross to be in some way central, and we may speak of them as the *mystical*, the *legal* and the *sacrificial* theories.

1. The *mystical* solution is perhaps the most fundamental. Paul sees mankind as 'in Adam'. Adam had disobeyed God in Eden, and so brought on his head the fate of dying; we are all involved in Adam's sin, and God's consequent punishment. How then are we to escape from this trap? By being transferred from the 'body of death' to the body of Christ, which is a body of life. 'For as by a man came death, by a man has come also the resurrection of the dead. For as in Adam all die, so in Christ shall all [who are in Christ] be made alive' (I Cor. 15.21f.). The transfer from one 'body' to the other takes place 'mystically' at baptism. When a Christian is baptized, he goes down under the water, which is a symbol of death; and when he comes up, it is into the new realm of life. He has been 'united' with Christ's death and resurrection.

> Do you not know that all of us who have been baptized into Christ Jesus were baptized into his death? We are buried therefore with him by baptism into death, so that as Christ was raised from the dead by the glory of the Father, we too might walk in newness of life. For if we have been united with him in a death like his, we shall certainly be united with him in a resurrection like his. We know that our old self was crucified with him so that the sinful body might be destroyed (Rom. 6.3–5).

Now this scheme of thinking can only work if we are being united with *Jesus Christ who was crucified*. In the possession christology it would not work. The aim would be to be united with the angelic Christ; but then the angelic Christ did not (could not) die, but left Jesus to die on the cross. Paul repeatedly stresses that Jesus Christ was a man: 'as by a man came death, *by a man* has come also the resurrection of the dead' (I Cor. 15.21); 'if many died through one man's trespass, much more have the grace of God and the free gift in the grace of *the one man* Jesus Christ abounded for many' (Rom. 5.15). The Pauline is thus united with Jesus Christ who is both a man who died, and also divine; so his baptism transfers him from being under God's judgment on all who are in Adam to the divine body of those who are in Christ.

We may well ask, How can a ceremony like baptism effect such a marvellous transfer? Paul just feels that the marvel is in Jesus Christ's death-and-resurrection, and that the transfer takes place in baptism by God's grace. It is a mystery; you cannot explain it. You just know that the end of the old age, the age 'in Adam', has begun because you know that Jesus has been resurrected. Jewish people thought of history as of limited length – six thousand years was sometimes mentioned – and the end would be like a mirror image of the beginning. Adam brought death: the end would bring return from death, resurrection. So Paul sees Jesus as a kind of second Adam: 'The first man was from the earth, a man of dust: the second man [Jesus Christ] is from heaven' (I Cor. 15.47). It wouldn't work if Jesus was not a man, like Adam; and it would not work if Jesus were *merely* a man – he is 'from heaven'.

Paul may express his mystical transfer theology more surprisingly than this:

> For our sake [God] made [Christ] to be sin who knew no sin, so that we might become the righteousness of God (II Cor. 5.21) Christ redeemed us from the curse of the law, having become a curse for us – for it is written, 'Cursed be everyone who hangs on a tree' – that in Christ Jesus the blessing of Abraham might come upon the Gentiles, that we might receive the promise of the Spirit through faith (Gal. 3.13f.).

He thinks of what we would call abstracts – sin, curse, righteousness, blessing – as 'things'. Christ who is sinless *becomes* sin so that we may *become* God's righteousness. There is a curse on everyone who does not keep the divine Law (Deut. 27.26; Gal. 3.10), and Christ has *become* a curse for us (by being crucified, there being a curse on 'everyone who hangs on a tree'); and the effect of this is that Gentiles are *not* cursed, but receive the blessing God promised to Abraham. Elsewhere Christ *became* for us wisdom from God, righteousness and sanctification and redemption (I Cor. 1.30); or 'he is our peace' (Eph. 2.14). But in every case the context is the cross, and Paul is interpreting Jesus' death as a means of transfer from our present plight to a glorious new life.

2. The second set of images which Paul uses is drawn from a *law-court*. The idea of God as judge was very old, and the sense of a divine judgment on human lives was developed across the Roman world; so such a picture was natural. There are some surprising features in it to our modern way of thinking, but it is not difficult to see how they have arisen.

Law-courts presuppose laws, and God has of course promulgated his Law in the Bible. But laws have to be enforced, and for this purpose kings employ what we would call a police force. Now policemen do various duties. They patrol their beat, and report or arrest any miscreants: we can all approve of that. But what are they to do with rebels like the IRA? They may subject them to prolonged questioning, and perhaps worse. Or they may join them covertly, and encourage them to drive into a police trap: that is called being an *agent provocateur*. These last activities are a cause of anxiety to the law-abiding: they may be justified, but they may not be, and the history of police forces is not reassuring. The experience which subject peoples had of the Roman imperial armies, which performed police duties, was not reassuring at all.

In the Old Testament God has an angel on the beat, whose job is to report to him any misdoings: he is called the Accuser, or in Hebrew the Satan. He is not a wicked angel *called* Satan. He is simply doing his job as a loyal angel, reporting on or accusing any criminal. God says to him, 'Where have you come from?', and he replies. 'From going to and fro on the earth, and from walking up and down on it' (Job 1.7). God boasts what a good man Job is, but the Satan suggests that Job may only be good for the reward he gets out of it; if God takes away some of his blessings – his flocks, his children, his health – he may curse God. God gives his permission, and so the Satan puts the screws on Job, as the Gestapo might put the screws on a suspect.

Suffering is always a problem to people of faith: if there is a loving God, why are we suffering? The answer of the Book of Job, 'God is allowing us to be tested, to see if we are really good', is not satisfying for long. Perhaps, comes the thought, God's angels are out of hand, like the Roman army. We may be accused of some trivial thing and flogged mercilessly, or crucified. Perhaps it is the same with God's angels; they are *malicious*, deliberately tormenting us, pleased to accuse us. By New Testament times their leader is a wicked angel *called Satan*. This is Paul's picture:

> What then shall we say to this? If God is for us, who is against us? He who did not spare his own Son but gave him up for us all, will he not also give us all things with him? Who shall bring any charge against God's elect? It is God who acquits; who is to condemn? It is Christ Jesus who died, yes, who was raised from the dead, who is at the right hand of God, who indeed pleads for us. Who shall separate us from the love of Christ? Shall tribulation, or distress, or persecution, or famine, or nakedness, or peril, or sword? . . . No, in all these things we are more than conquerors through him who loved us. For I am persuaded that neither death, nor life, nor angels, nor principalities . . . will be able to separate us from the love of God in Christ Jesus our Lord (Rom. 8.31–39).

Christians have been experiencing persecution (5.3), and Paul sees this as the activity of the angels and principalities, the heavenly police force; as with Job, they are trying the Christians out to see if they are strong in the faith – perhaps some have recanted. Paul is persuaded that no such sufferings will make the Roman church give up their faith, and so separate them from Christ. But what about the court of Judgment? Will these angels not be there *laying* accusations to *the charge of God's elect*? Indeed they will: but we have nothing to fear. For we have Christ there to *plead for us*, and he is *God's Son, God gave him up for us all*, so naturally he means to *acquit* us. With Christ there as our defending lawyer, we shall surely be all right: *will he not also give us all things with him?*

It is to be noticed that again the argument only works if Jesus Christ is both human and divine. If he were not human he could not have *died* for us, and it is the dying, the fact that he was not *spared but given up for us all* which makes his *pleading* unanswerable. But this would not be so if he were a mere man: it is because he is *God's Son* that there is a total change in the divine law-court. The possessionist christology would not work here either; for on the Jerusalem theory the angelic Christ had not died and the human Jesus was a mere man.

Paul presses the same point in Colossians:

For in [Christ] the whole fullness of deity dwells bodily . . . And you, who were dead in trespasses and the uncircumcision of your flesh, God made alive together with him, having forgiven us our trespasses, having cancelled the bond which stood against us with its legal rulings; this he set aside, nailing it to the cross. He disarmed the principalities and powers, and made a public example of them, triumphing over them in it (Col. 2.9, 13–15).

The thought behind *God made you alive together with Christ* is the mystical transfer I discussed under (1) above. With our *trespasses* we were *dead* in the sense that we were bound into the body of Adam who trespassed and died, and if nothing were done we should go to eternal death; but baptism is a symbolic resurrection, and *makes us alive together with Christ*. But Paul moves on then to the divine Law-court. God has *forgiven us our trespasses*: but how can he do that if he is just? The divine Law was *a bond which stood against us* – and not only the biblical Law but the *legal rulings* made by Jewish experts. All these things we have broken, and the *principalities and powers* – that is the senior angels – are waiting to accuse us before God's throne. Would a just God not inevitably condemn us? No, replies the apostle: God has *set the Law aside*, abolished it, *nailed it to the cross*. The Law was the weapon of *the principalities and powers*, and God has *disarmed them*. They were our malicious accusers, and God has treated them as a Roman general treats his conquered enemies: he has *made a public example of them, triumphing over them in the cross*. In a Roman triumph the chief prisoners were led in chains behind the conqueror in his chariot, and then executed.

Once more we see the necessity of something more than possessionism. They thought at Jerusalem that the dying Jesus was just a man: how could the death of a good man secure the abolition of the divine Law? But if *the whole fullness of deity dwelt in* Jesus Christ, then matters take on a different complexion: God may waive the Law if his Son has died for us and asks him, his Son *in whom the whole fullness of deity dwelt bodily*.

3. In occasional sentences Paul speaks of Jesus' death as a *sacrifice*, comparing it to various of the Old Testament sacrifices. Paul was

taught at his conversion that 'Christ died for our sins in accordance with the scriptures' (I Cor. 15.3): perhaps the meaning is that the Bible requires sacrifice when we sin, and the cross was already seen as a sacrifice. Paul himself says that God sent 'his own Son in the likeness of sinful flesh and as a sin-offering' (Rom. 8.3); and that 'God put [Christ] forward as an expiation by his blood' (Rom. 3.25). Jews felt that if they had broken one of God's commandments there was a barrier between them and him, and the only thing they could do, other than repenting, was to *expiate* the sin by the *blood* of an animal. How then could the sin of the whole world be expiated. God is just, and cannot just wink at our rebellions. He *put forward* his own Son *as an expiation* 'to show [his] righteousness . . . to prove that he himself is righteous and that he acquits him who has faith in Jesus' (3.26). So forgiveness has not been on the cheap, God has insisted on an expiation for sin as he would if we were providing it, he has given his own Son as the expiation, and so he may with justice *acquit us.*

Later on the Paulines expatiated on this theme. Hebrews especially gives a third of the book to the idea of Christ as our high priest offering his death to God 'for the remission of sins'; and in the Fourth Gospel the Baptist sees Jesus as 'the lamb of God who takes away the sin of the world' (John 1.29). But the basic idea is not quite satisfactory. Jews thought that sin-offerings could be made only for *unintentional* sins, as when a motorist might kill a child. If you sinned 'with a high hand', you could not just pay a sacrifice and get out of it: David murdered Uriah, and he said properly, 'Thou hast no delight in sacrifice' (Ps. 51.16). Such sins were coped with by the scapegoat which was taken to the desert and killed on Atonement Day. But the scapegoat was not sacrificed, and Christ is never compared to a scapegoat. Paul's more fundamental thought is of the mystical transfer and of the abolition of the Law by the cross; the sacrificial images are just occasional, taken over from earlier Christian attempts to make sense of the cross.

So whichever way Paul's thought moved, it seemed clear that the possession theory would not work. God had called him, Paul, to carry to the Gentiles the good news that they were saved from a destiny of eternal death, destruction or torment. This could be understood as a mystical transfer from being in Adam to being in

Christ; or as the revocation of the Law that would condemn them, through the pleading of God's crucified Son; or as a universal kind of sacrifice. But in every case the cross was the key; and in every case it was required that Jesus Christ had been a divine as well as a human being. What was required was incarnation.

20

Lord and Son of God

It is one thing to *need* incarnation, and another to *prove* that it has taken place; and proving here means finding texts for it in the Old Testament. What the Paulines in fact did was to keep their ears open when they heard the Bible read, and especially when they sang the Psalms; and it was on the narrow base of (effectively) three Psalms that they felt they were able to construct proofs of their incarnation christology.

One of the earliest texts to be noticed was Ps. 110.1:

The Lord said to my Lord, Sit at my right hand, Until I make your enemies a footstool for your feet.

The wording seems a little confusing, but the original meaning, in the Old Testament, is not too difficult. God [*The Lord*] promises the Israelite ruler [*my Lord*] victory over his *enemies*: the Israelite ruler is *sitting* on a throne, perhaps at a coronation ceremony to the *right* side of the Temple (viewed from God's angle). But the Christian singer thinks of the verse as referring to Jesus Christ: he is *my Lord*. Now Jesus can only be thought of as *sitting at God's right hand* in heaven, following his resurrection; and the *enemies* will then be the angelic *principalities and powers* whom I discussed in the last chapter. So it must have seemed a marvellous text. It 'foretold' the resurrection (understood) and Jesus' consequent enthronement in heaven (which we otherwise would not have known about); and God's intention shortly to defeat and humiliate the powers who oppress us in this world (which is good news indeed). Furthermore it gives Jesus the very highest honour: he is not only *my Lord*, but has been given the throne alongside God's in heaven, and the powers are to be put under *his* feet. This is no ordinary man, temporarily possessed by an angelic spirit.

This is the sense which we find Paul giving to the verse from early years:

> For [Christ] must reign [in heaven] till he *puts* all his *enemies* under *his feet* (I Cor. 15.25).

The chapter is about the resurrection, and Paul is answering the question, How then does Jesus' physical resurrection fit in with ours? Answer: his is like the first sheaf of the harvest, which (it so happens) was offered in the Temple a couple of days after Passover – we shall be the full harvest. In the end Christ will hand the kingdom over to God the Father, when the angelic enemies have all been reduced to obedience. In Rom. 8.34 similarly:

> Christ who died, or rather was raised, who is also at *the right hand* of God.

The resurrection again leads on to an echo of Ps. 110; and the verses following, which I cited in the last chapter, speak of the inability of the *principalities and powers* to separate Christians from the love of God. Or again Eph. 1.20 reads:

> which he accomplished in Christ when he raised him from the dead and made him *sit at his right hand* in the heavenly realm.

Paul's disciples followed his lead. Hebrews, written soon after Paul's death, asks:

> To which of the angels has [God] ever said, *Sit at my right hand, till I make your enemies a footstool for your feet?* (1.13).

The position is so exalted that it is clearly intended for one higher than the angelic powers championed by the Jerusalem mission. Twenty years later Luke is writing an ideal sermon for Peter at Pentecost, and puts into his mouth the words (Acts 2.29–34):

Men and brethren, I may say frankly to you about the patriarch David that he both died and was buried . . . For David did not go up to heaven, but he himself says, *The Lord said to my Lord, sit at my right hand until I make your enemies a footstool for your feet.*

By Luke's time the question has been asked, What makes you so sure that these words are about Jesus? Are they not spoken by the court poet 'For David' in the heading of the psalm, and therefore about him? No, replies Luke, that cannot be right: as we all know David died and his tomb was visible in Jerusalem – the text is about the one who *has* gone up to heaven by the resurrection, and that is Jesus.

There is actually no reason why Peter should not have spoken these words at Pentecost (though Luke gives the exact Greek version of the Psalm, and Peter would have been speaking Aramaic). But by the 60s the battle had moved on, and Pauline Christians like Mark used the text to challenge the Petrine teaching that Christ was merely the human descendant of David. Jesus asks:

How do the scribes say that Christ is the son of David? For David himself said in the Holy Spirit, *The Lord said to my Lord, Sit at my right hand until I put your enemies* beneath *your feet.* David himself calls him *Lord*, so how is he his son? (Mark 12.35 ff.)

Mark is carrying the war into enemy territory. The Jerusalem Christians included scribes among their leaders (Matt. 23.34). Paulines are scandalized by their hopelessly inadequate christology (shared no doubt by non-Christian Jewish scribes), and use Ps. 110.1 as an argument for their own Incarnation view. David is now understood to be the *author* of the psalm (the whole *book* is referred to as 'The Psalms of David'). If he *wrote* the psalm, then he spoke of the person addressed as *My Lord*. But (in Jewish practice, now, alas, felt to be out of date) children respected their parents, not vice versa; no ancestor could speak of his descendant as his *Lord*. So Christ must be a *divine* figure, no mere human descendant of David.

The title *Lord* is in fact tricky. The Hebrew word *'Adon(ai)* is used for both God and human masters, and so is the Greek *kyrios*. In the Bible God is often spoken of by his name Yahweh, and for reverence

Jews do not speak this name, but say '*Adonai* (our Lord); so when the
Greek translators of the Old Testament came to the name, they
simply put *ho kyrios* (the Lord), and this survives into the traditional
English translations with capitals, *the* LORD. People no doubt
addressed Jesus by the respectful *Lord* in his lifetime, and after his
death we know that the Aramaic-speaking church, that is the
Jerusalem church, used the short prayer *Marana tha*, Our Lord,
come (I Cor. 16.22). But there is a step between *addressing* someone
as Lord and *describing* them *as the Lord*: Matthew often has the
address, but Luke moves over to the description. *Lord* is in fact what
is sometimes called an escalator-word: it goes up in significance
while apparently remaining still. Paul often speaks of 'the Lord
(Jesus Christ)', and he is quite happy (more than happy) to use as of
Christ Old Testament texts which speak of God as 'the Lord'. So
the Paulines had an invaluable tool to hand. Old Testament texts
which spoke of the Lord, meaning God, could be understood to
mean Jesus; and the more Jesus was spoken of as 'the Lord', the
closer he was to divinity.

A famous instance of this transfer of *Lord* from God to Christ
comes in Philippians. Isaiah had said, in God's name:

I, the LORD, speak the truth . . . I am God, and there is no other.
By myself have I sworn, from my mouth has gone forth in
righteousness a word that shall not return. To me every knee shall
bow, every tongue confess (45.19, 22f.).

Paul is describing how Christ Jesus was on an equality with God, but
emptied himself and became a man, and died on the cross; and he
ends:

Therefore God has highly exalted him and bestowed on him the
name which is above every name, that at the name of Jesus *every
knee should bow*, in heaven and on earth and under the earth, and
every tongue confess that Jesus Christ is *Lord*, to the glory of God
the Father (Phil. 2.9–11).

In Isaiah the knees were to bow to *God*, and the tongues were to
confess *God*; but in Paul these acts of worship are directed to Jesus

Christ. Because of his self-giving God has given him *the name which is above every name*, that is the name *Lord*. It was the LORD speaking in the prophecy, and that name now belongs to Jesus. Escalators are marvellous: you have moved up a floor without noticing it.

A second title which appealed to the Paulines was 'the Son of God'. This phrase comes occasionally in the Old Testament, and it has different meanings. Sometimes the angels are called sons of God, as when, on the day of creation 'the morning stars sang together, and all the sons of God shouted for joy' (Job 38.7). Sometimes God's people Israel is spoken of as his son: the most famous instance is when the prophet Hosea says about the Exodus, 'Out of Egypt I called my son' (Hos. 11.1). But the most significant use is when the Israelite king is spoken of as God's son; and here again it was a Psalm text which proved to be the catalyst.

In Ps. 2 the Israelite king is the speaker, and he describes the kings and rulers of the nations as 'taking counsel together against the Lord and his anointed' (*Christ*, in Greek). He appeals to the promise which God made long ago to David through Nathan:

> I will tell of the decree of the Lord: He said to me, You are my son, today I have begotten you (Ps. 2.7).

It was believed that God had promised that David's dynasty should be kings of Israel *for ever* – unlike Saul's family: God had said of each of his descendants, 'I will be to him a father, and he shall be to me a son' (II Sam. 7. 14). So that was *the decree of the Lord*. The new king then inherits this position at his coronation, and becomes *God's son*. So although he may be twenty-five years of age, he has only just become God's son, and it is said, rather uncomfortably perhaps, *today I have begotten you*.

Here was a happy coincidence for the Paulines: it would be common ground for all Christians that *his Christ* meant Jesus, but it was evident that this Christ was also spoken of as God's *Son* – and that must seem to imply a unique relationship. In early days of persecution the psalm is said by Luke to have been quoted as a prophecy now fulfilled (Acts 4.25–27): Herod was a *king* and Pontius Pilate was a *ruler*, and they had acted together against God and Jesus, *his Anointed.* But it is not till Paul preaches, in Acts 13.33, that we have the application of v. 7:

> And we bring you the good news that what God promised to the fathers, this he has fulfilled to us their children by raising Jesus; as also it is written in the second psalm, *You are my Son, today I have begotten you.*

The interesting, and surprising, thing is that the text is applied to the *resurrection* of Jesus, not to his conception – *by raising Jesus.* But this is not really such a surprise. Nobody knew about Jesus' conception; everyone in the church believed in his resurrection. This was God's supreme act in vindicating Jesus: it was therefore understood as the today when he had become God's Son, when God had, so to speak, *begotten him.*

We have to be careful about what Luke says Paul said; but in this instance we have Paul saying the same thing himself. In the opening verses of Romans Paul is speaking about the gospel:

> the gospel of God which he promised beforehand through his prophets in the holy scriptures, the gospel concerning his Son, who was descended from David according to the flesh and designated Son of God in power according to the Spirit of holiness by his resurrection from the dead, Jesus Christ our Lord (Rom. 1.3f.).

The gospel is said by Paul to have been *promised beforehand in the holy scriptures,* in this case Ps. 2, which does *concern his Son.* It speaks of God's *Anointed, his Christ,* which implies (following the Nathan oracle in II Sam. 7) that Jesus *was descended from David according to the flesh;* but he is also *designated Son of God,* because Ps. 2 speaks of *the decree, You are my Son, today I have begotten you.* So Paul really did use Ps. 2 as a text, and he really did think that the *today* referred to Easter. The double descent, both from David and from God, is left a mystery: the one is *according to the flesh* and the other *according to the Spirit of holiness.*

With time Ps. 2.7 was allowed its more natural meaning: Jesus was God's Son from eternity, not just from the resurrection. Hebrews is intent on proving the Jerusalem mission wrong, with their angelic possession theory, and begins:

> God . . . has in these last days spoken to us by a Son, whom he appointed heir of all things, through whom also he created the world . . . For to what angel did God ever say, *You are my Son, today I have begotten you?* (Heb. 1.1–3).

Jesus Christ is God's eternal *Son* now, and it was *through him* that God *created the world*: the Psalm text is there to prove his Sonship, and the *today* has slipped back into eternity. Its polemical value has now become much clearer too. The Jerusalem Christians taught that an angelic power called Christ had taken hold of Jesus at his Baptism: the Pauline author of Hebrews replies, 'To what angel did God ever say, You are my Son?' A Son is in a different category from an angel.

We have seen that the Ebionite Gospel actually makes an attempt to deploy the same text. Mark had hinted – accidentally, as I should say – that something crucial happened at Jesus' Baptism, for there God said to him, *You are my* beloved *Son* (Mark 1.11). The Ebionites – that is, the Jerusalem Christians half a century on – added, *'today I have begotten you'*. In their view the Spirit/Christ entered Jesus neither at his resurrection nor in eternity, but at his Baptism. It was then that the angelic possession began.

Other Christians turned the text over in their minds, and still another suggestion arose. If Jesus is God's Son, and God was his Father ('Abba'), the question must arise sooner or later, How then was he conceived? It was not Joseph who fathered him, God did; and we cannot think of God as giving conception to a human man's wife, in some unspeakable kind of divine adultery. Surely the mother must have been a virgin girl. But, thinks St Matthew, is that not exactly what God foretold in the [Greek] Bible? Did not Isaiah say, 'Behold, a virgin shall conceive and bear a son, and his name shall be called Emmanuel [God-with-us]' (Isa. 7.14)? So we have the beginning of the virginal conception doctrine: Jesus was God's Son neither from Easter nor from the baptism, but from Lady Day.

The Son of Man

It is fairly easy to understand why the Paulines should have wished to speak of Jesus as Lord or Son of God. The matter is not so easy with a third title, *the Son of Man*, which is far more common than either of these in the Synoptic Gospels. The problem has been so acute that a vast amount has been written about it, and I am going about the discussion of it in a rather different way from the rest of this book.

'Son of man' (*ben 'adam* in Hebrew) is a not uncommon phrase in the Old Testament, and it means, uncomplicatedly, a male human being. God says to Ezekiel, 'Prophesy to the wind, prophesy, son of man' (Ezek. 37.9): God is speaking to a human being, and he calls him 'son of man'. 'What is man that thou art mindful of him?', wonders the psalmist, 'Or the son of man that thou carest for him?' (Ps. 8.4). Hebrew poetry often repeats the same idea in a second line: here *the son of man* means exactly the same as *man*. 'And behold, with the clouds of heaven came one like a son of man' (Dan. 7.13). Daniel has seen a vision of a series of beasts – a lion, a bear, a leopard and a wild beast – and now he sees a figure like a human being, *one like a son of man*. The Daniel chapter is written in Aramaic, not Hebrew, but the idea is just the same: the phrase just means *man*, and it is used when man is contrasted either with God or with animals.

The phrases *a son of man* (*bar ('e)nash* in Aramaic), and *the son of man* (*bar nasha* in Aramaic) are not uncommon in Jewish writings of the early centuries AD. Here are a few examples from those published by Professor Vermes:[1]

---

[1]Geza Vermes, 'The Use of בר נשא/בר נש in Jewish Aramaic', Appendix E in Matthew Black, *An Aramaic Approach to the Gospels and Acts* third edition, Oxford 1967, 310–330.

All sweat proceeding from a son of man is deadly poison.

Whoever says, Here are five (pieces of money), give me something worth three, is a fool. But he who speaks thus, Here are three, give me something worth five – he is a son of man.

Rabbi Ze'ira wished to buy a pound of meat from a butcher. How much is this? he asked. Fifty minas and a lash, was the answer. (The Rabbi offered 60, 70, 80, and finally 100 minas to escape the lash, but to no avail. In the end he said), Do as is your custom! In the evening, he went to the school-house and said, Rabbis, how wicked is the custom of this place that a son of man cannot eat a pound of meat until he has been given a lash!

Rabbi Simeon ben Yohai hid in a cave for 13 years (during Hadrian's persecution; he came out at last and saw a bird escape a hunter's net). He then said, Not even a bird perishes without the will of Heaven: how much less the son of man!

All these instances come from the Palestinian Talmud, a compendium of Jewish traditions collected from the first four centuries AD. It should be noticed that both *a son of man* and *the son of man* are used, but in the same sense. In the last story *the son of man* could be replaced by *a man* (compare *a bird* in the previous sentence).

So what about the use of the phrase in the Gospels? Jesus often says things like, 'Foxes have holes but the Son of man has nowhere to lay his head', or 'The Son of man has authority on earth to forgive sins'; and it can be seen at once that the use is quite different from those we have been looking at. *The Son of man* is clearly being used here as a kind of title, and it refers to Jesus, and him alone; we could not replace it with *a man* without changing the meaning, but we could replace it with *the Son of God*. So the idea became widespread that *the Son of Man* was a title in use among Jews in Jesus' time: people were expecting the Son of Man to come, as they were expecting the Christ, and Jesus was announcing that he was this Son of Man. You notice that capitals have crept in: no longer *the son of man*, but *the Son of Man*.

There are three things wrong with this theory, and it is now generally in retreat. First, we have enough evidence, from the Bible and from Jewish writings that *the son of man* was a phrase quite widely used, and that it had a general meaning which everyone would have understood. In English we have (less dignified) expressions for a man, like *chap* or *bloke*; and if a new leader began referring to himself as *the Chap* or *the Bloke*, people would be mystified.

Second, there is a curious gap in the New Testament evidence. St Paul never uses the phrase, nor does it come in any of the other epistles; nor does anyone else but Jesus use it in the Gospels. The contrast with other titles shows how peculiar this is. The Jews send to John Baptist to ask him, 'Who are you?', and he says, 'I am not the Christ'. They continue, 'What then? are you Elijah? . . . Are you the prophet?' (John 1. 19–21). There are various expected figures, and *the Son of Man* does not seem to be one of them. Peter says to Jesus, 'You are the Christ!', and that is obviously important, but no one ever says, 'You are the Son of Man!', or 'Can this be the Son of Man?'

Third, the evidence which was once thought to support the idea of *the Son of Man* as a title has come to look very shaky. There is a document known as *The Parables (Similitudes) of Enoch* (I Enoch 37–71), which is usually thought to come from the same sort of time as the Gospels, and the phrase seems to be used there about a human figure in heaven to whom God entrusts the judgment of mankind. However, the work is preserved in Ethiopic, and the translation may be questioned; and it seems that Enoch is being told about 'that son of man' who will do the judging, and who afterwards turns out to be him himself. So there is no title *The Son of Man* in evidence there. Still less is there, as was often said, a figure in Dan. 7 in the Bible called the Son of Man: I have cited the verse above, and it speaks of *one like a son of man*. So the idea of *The Son of Man* as a title of a heavenly being expected in the first century collapses.

A different theory has been popular in recent years, proposed for example by Barnabas Lindars in England and Mogens Müller in Denmark. Jesus, on this view, used the expression *the son of man* in the normal sense, and everyone understood him so. He meant 'Foxes have holes and birds have nests, but men have nowhere to lay their heads' – me, for example. Or he meant, 'Men have authority to pronounce sins forgiven'; the theory is on firmer ground here because in Matthew's version the story ends with the crowd glorifying God 'who had given such authority to *men*' (Matt. 9.8). When he said, 'The son of man goes as it is written of him, but woe to that man by whom the son of man is betrayed' (Mark 14.21), Jesus meant 'Man dies, as the Bible said of Adam, but woe to him by whom a man is betrayed'. In each case *the son of man* would have a general meaning, but would have reference to the speaker, rather like R. Simeon and the bird.

This theory is more plausible than the first one, but I do not find it convincing. The evangelists who give us the sayings are for the most part Mark and Matthew; and Mark and Matthew spoke Aramaic, and will have been familiar with the meaning of common Aramaic idioms. They think that *the Son of Man* is a title by which Jesus referred to himself, not a general expression for mankind. The three instances which I have given above are selected: in these cases a general sense can be given, and meaning survives; but in most instances this is not so. Jesus often speaks of 'the Son of Man coming' or says that the Son of Man will be three days and three nights in the belly of the earth; and these sayings can only mean that he, Jesus, will come back to earth, or will be buried three days before being resurrected. So what is implied is that over the preponderance of the sayings two evangelists whose mother-tongue was Aramaic totally misunderstood a common idiom, and that they preserve sayings for which that idiom does not make sense. We need to do better than that.

We are better to think in terms of the battle between the Paulines and the Jerusalem mission. We have seen that the crucial titles *Lord* and *Son of God* were discovered in the Psalms, and there is a third short psalm which is also much cited from early times. I have mentioned it already:

What is man that you are mindful of him:
Or the son of man that you care for him?
You made him a little lower than the angels.
You crowned him with glory and honour,
You put everything in subjection under his feet (Ps. 8.4–6).

The Petrines were keen on the activities of the angelic powers, and Paul was wanting to put the latter down. So when, as we saw, Paul was discussing the resurrection, he refers to Ps. 110.1 saying that Christ will deliver the kingdom to God when he has *put* all *his enemies* under *his feet* (I Cor. 15.24f.). Psalm 110 promised to make the king's enemies *a footstool* for his feet, but the similar phrase *under his feet* slips in by association from Ps. 8.6. Paul then goes on at 15.27 to cite Ps. 8.6, 'For God *put all things in subjection under his feet*'; to prove that Christ will have *all* his angelic enemies subjected to him.

There is a similar move in Eph. 1.20ff. God raised Christ from the dead and made him *sit at his right hand* in heaven, following Ps. 110.1, putting him above every principality and power – i.e. *his enemies* from Ps. 110.1 – and *he put all things in subjection under his feet*, following Ps. 8.6. In Ps. 110 he made them a footstool for his feet, but the phrasing from Ps. 8 comes to mind, and Paul is feeling less threatened and more genial at the end of his life. He does not call the powers *enemies* now, nor make them a *footstool*: Christ is just *above* them, and they are *in subjection under his feet*, which is quite humiliating enough.

A few years later Paul was dead, and the writer to the Hebrews took the torch over. He gives his first two chapters to a long series of texts proving that angels are inferior to God's Son, Jesus, and he ends by citing Ps. 8.4–6, the three verses. He then explains their meaning:

> Now in *putting everything in subjection* to him, he left nothing unsubjected. As it is, we do not yet see *everything in subjection* to him. But we see Jesus, who *for a little while was made lower than the angels, crowned with glory and honour* because of the suffering of death, so that by the grace of God he might taste death for everyone (Heb. 2.5–9).

The modern reader might well be astonished. The psalmist was talking about *man, the son of man*, that is human beings at large: God made them lower than angels, but they are the kings of creation down here; the *all things* which are subject to them are the animals, *all sheep and oxen*, as the psalm goes on to say. But to the early Christians this was about Jesus, and it was a godsend – indeed a God-send: for it seemed to yield the central Pauline theology in opposition to the Petrines.

That this should be so was partly due to an accident in the Greek Old Testament translation. The Hebrew says a *little* lower than the angels; but the Greek translation (*brachu ti*) can mean *for a little while*;

and this is how Hebrews takes it. So Jesus was an eternal being who *was made for a little while lower than the angels* so much talked of by the Petrines: that is the doctrine of the *incarnation* – he had been higher than the angels eternally, but for the period of his earthly life he was lower. He *was crowned with glory and honour*: that is his resurrection and enthronement in heaven. *All things have been subjected to him:* that is his ultimate victory over the powers. But God can only have *crowned him with glory* in recognition of something he has done: that is the *cross*, where he *tasted death for everyone*. The verses cover the incarnation, the atonement, the resurrection and the kingdom: who could ask for more? Well, there is more. They also tell us an important title of Jesus: he was *the Son of Man*.

The title was important to the Paulines, and they exploited it. The Jerusalem mission taught that the human Jesus was possessed by a heavenly *spirit*: but to the Paulines Jesus-Christ was an eternal unity, both a spirit and in some way human. This seemed to be paradoxical: how useful then to discover that one of the titles of the pre-existent Lord was *the Son of Man*! That made quite self-evident his eternal humanity, and so confounded the opposition. There was a tendency therefore to put the phrase into Jesus' mouth, especially in sayings with the same force as the Hebrews passage just cited. For instance:

> The Son of Man must suffer many things, and be rejected by the elders and the chief priests and the scribes, and be killed, and after three days rise again (Mark 8.31; cf. 9.31, 10.33f.).

The church has put a 'prophecy' on Jesus' lips with details of the different Jewish authorities (and at 10.33f., the mocking, spitting and scourging): but the outline is what is said in Ps. 8, as understood in Heb. 2 – Jesus is the eternal *Son of Man*, he is destined to *suffer death*, but beyond that stands his rising again to *glory*. We should notice the important little word *must* in Mark 8.31: Mark knows it *must* happen because God has foretold it for us in scripture, and the scripture is Ps. 8.4–6.

Once *the Son of Man* has been seen by the Paulines to be significant, the Daniel passage came to mind, where *one like a son of man came with the clouds*, and God gave him all authority (Dan. 7.13f.). Jesus had been taken to heaven, and Jesus had been given all authority (*all things subject under his feet*), and Jesus Christ was *the Son of Man*: so the passage was obviously about him. In Daniel the *one like a son of man* (who is a symbol of the Jewish people in face of the beastly empires) is brought *up* to the divine throne with the clouds; but then that suggests how in the end Christ will come and establish his kingdom on earth. There were no Christians present at Jesus' trial, so Mark imagines the High priest demanding if he was the Christ. Jesus answers:

I am; and you will see *the Son of Man* seated at the right hand of Power, and *coming with the clouds of heaven* (Mark. 14.62).

The Marcan church has combined Ps. 110.1, *seated at the right hand* of Power, with Dan. 7.13, *the Son of Man coming with the clouds of heaven*. The Daniel text has often provided the inspiration for Pauline visions of Christ's return:

of him will *the Son of Man* be ashamed when *he comes* in the glory of his Father with the holy angels (Mark 8.38).

Then will they see *the Son of Man coming in clouds* with great power and glory (Mark 13.26).

The authority element was important too. The Paulines were maintaining that much of the Law no longer applied, and they needed authority for so bold a teaching. How could Jesus revoke the Fourth Commandment? Well:

The Son of Man is lord even of the sabbath (Mark. 2.28).

How can Christians dispense with the Jewish sacrifices? Well:

The Son of Man has authority on earth to forgive sins (Mark 2.10).

The title was very congenial to the Paulines, and comes about seventy times in the Gospels.

So, to sum up: Jesus never used the title *the Son of Man* of himself.

If he used the phrase at all, it would have been in the sense ordinary people used it, to mean *a man*. That is why it never occurs in Paul, or the other Epistles. But it did come in Ps. 8.4–6; and Paul, and later more fully Hebrews, applied the text to Jesus: it seemed to speak of his incarnation, death and resurrection, and victorious enthronement. This opened the way for Mark, and later the other evangelists. *The Son of Man* now appeared as the title of a pre-existent human spiritual being, who *was made for a little while lower than the angels*. The similar text in Dan. 7.13 suggested applying the title to Jesus' second coming, and to the authority which God had given him. So there is the solution to a long-standing enigma: the Two Missions hypothesis is a master-key to open every lock.

22

The Limits of Monotheism

Jewish people sometimes ask, 'How could a Jew like Paul, who believed that there was only one God, speak of Jesus as his Son, and accord him divine honours?'; and it is a sensible question. But in fact many Jews had for centuries felt absolute monotheism to be a strain. It seemed rather simple to think of 'the LORD God walking in the garden in the cool of the day' (Gen. 3.10), or in fact of doing anything directly. So they spoke of the hand of the LORD, the arm of the LORD, the Spirit of God, the Word of God, and such expressions; and in time these ideas were thought of not just as poetry, but as real extensions of God. For instance in Prov. 8.22–30 in the Bible, Wisdom speaks of herself as God's first creation and master-workman in the making of the world, a kind of archangel: and divine Wisdom is very close to divinity.

We have many writings from a Jew called Philo who lived in Alexandria at about the same time as St Paul; and Philo tells us that this Wisdom has many names, two of which are (to us surprisingly) Beginning and Image (*Allegory of the Laws* 1.43). In another place he speaks of the Word (Greek *Logos*) as God's first-born 'who holds the eldership among the angels, their ruler as it were; and many names are his, for he is called Beginning, and the Name of God, and his Word, and the Man after his Image' (*Confusion of Tongues* 146). These comments show that God was felt too exalted to act directly in the world, and that a lot of study had been devoted to the first chapters of the Bible, to try to find out what angelic powers had actually been involved in its creation. For the Bible was God's revelation to man, and the truth would be hidden there somewhere if one looked hard enough.

In Gen. 1.26 'God said, Let us make man . . .' – let *us* make man:

so he was not creating the world on his own, and the presence of angelic beings seemed already to be implied. Now Gen. 1.1 reads in our translations, 'In the beginning God created . . .'; but the Hebrew word for *in* (*be-*) can also mean *by*. So came the suggestion that God created the world by means of an archangel called *Beginning*. Of course this is fanciful, but we can understand it, and it explains Philo's 'first-born who holds the eldership among the angels . . . called Beginning'. We may also notice that this archangel is sometimes called *the Word*: one of the psalms says, 'By the word of the Lord were the heavens made' (Ps. 33.6), and creation took place when God *said*, Let there be light. So again there was a Genesis text for thinking that the world was made through a kind of extension of God, in this case called the Word.

One of the complications of the creation story is that there are two accounts of the creation of man, one in Gen. 1.27 and the other in 2.7: the first tells of man being made in God's image, and made 'male and female', while the second speaks of God forming man out of clay, and breathing into him the breath of life. To us this is evidence of two different stories (P and JE); but Philo did not think in these terms, and he has his own explanation. The first creation, in Gen. 1.27, is of a spiritual being in heaven, a combination of the two sexes, and is spoken of as the *Image*, or *the Man after the Image*, while the second is Adam, the man of flesh, our ancestor. To Philo the phrase 'in/by (Heb *be-*) our Image' was an indication that the archangel was being referred to, and so this was another name for him.

When it came to the push, Philo was a monotheist: he believed there was one God, the cardinal point of Jewish faith, and that these supposed beings derived from the Genesis text were names of an archangel. But he uses exalted language about them – they are 'God's first-born', and the Word is spoken of as divine (Greek *theos*, but not *ho theos*). I have also mentioned the visionary tradition in Judaism about this time, and there too we find a tendency to see 'powers in heaven' alongside God (as in *The Life of Adam and Eve*). Among the Dead Sea Scrolls too, a passage was found in Cave 11 speaking of the angel Melchisedek by the word *'Elohim* (God). So we may think of extensions of God being spoken of quite widely, without any intention to infringe God's prerogative.

Towards the end of his life Paul found the issue of christology becoming more acute. The Petrines spoke of some angel or spirit which had possessed Jesus, and Paul denies this forcibly: 'In him the fullness of God was pleased to dwell . . . in him the whole fullness of deity dwells bodily' (Col. 1.19, 2.9). He draws on the same traditions which we have noticed in Philo to expound this:

> He is the image of the invisible God, the first-born of all creation; for in him were all things created, in heaven and on earth, visible and invisible, whether thrones or dominions or principalities or authorities – all things were created through him and for him. He is before all things, and in him all things hold together. He is the head of the body, the church; he is the beginning, the first-born from the dead, that in everything he might be pre-eminent (Col. 1.15–18).

In the background lie claims by Petrine visionaries to have been rapt to heaven, and there to have seen the various angelic powers: that is why Paul stresses that God is *invisible*, and speaks a little sharply about creation *visible and invisible*; and why he refers to the different classes of angels – *whether thrones or dominions or principalities or powers*. He is distrustful of the visionaries' pretensions to have been up to heaven at all, and of their claims to know one lot of heavenly powers from another. But reports we have from later Jewish visionaries do regularly describe the different orders of angels, beginning with the Throne-angels; and it is against such a background that Paul is writing.

What he objects to most is the suggestion that the earthly Jesus was merely the temporary possession of one of these powers. On the contrary, *he is the Image of God*: he is the primary power in heaven, and he exists from before creation, its *First-born*. He is the Image of Gen. 1.26f., and all the angelic orders were created after him, and by his mediation, and for his benefit – *through him and for him*. So all the things which were said about Wisdom in Proverbs 8 apply to him. Paul is not content even to leave it that the pre-existent Christ was the first heavenly power, the archangel. *In him all the fullness of God was pleased to dwell*. It was thought that God's *fullness* extended to all heaven, and that many powers partook of his glory. No, says Paul: all the fullness was concentrated in Christ alone.

Christ's pre-eminence leads on to a second thought. He is the head, too, to *the church* in this world: that is to say, the church is like a human *body*, and Christ both fills it, in the same way that the fullness of God dwells in him, and is also over against it as its *head*. But then this leads back to the Genesis idea again: *head* and *beginning* are the same root in Hebrew (*ro'sh/re'shith*), and so Christ is also the Beginning of Gen. 1.1 by which God made heaven and earth. And he is the *first-born from the dead* too, by virtue of his resurrection. So in every way Jesus Christ is pre-eminent and no mere angel possessing a mere man.

Colossians shows Paul wrestling with the mystery of who Christ was. He was certainly not the prophet of the Jerusalem christology, taken over by the Spirit. But nor is he the Second Person of the Trinity. He is the archangel called Image or Wisdom or Beginning. Paul does not call him God, but he does say that the whole fullness of deity dwelt in him bodily; and that opened the gate to deity in time.

In Paul's last letter, Philippians, he takes the matter up again:

Have this mind among yourselves which is yours in Christ Jesus, who, though he was in the form of God, did not count equality with God a thing to be grasped, but emptied himself, taking the form of a slave, being born in the likeness of men. And being found in human form he humbled himself and became obedient unto death, even death on a cross. Therefore God has highly exalted him and bestowed on him the name which is above every name, that at the name of Jesus every knee should bow, in heaven and on earth and under the earth, and every tongue confess that Jesus Christ is Lord, to the glory of God the Father (Phil. 2.5–11).

Paul wants the Philippians to live together in harmony and *humility*; Christ *humbled himself* when he left heaven and came to earth, and as they are Christians they already *have this mind in Christ Jesus* and should live up to it. But the present disharmonies give him an opportunity to expound his christological belief, which is still being developed.

As in Colossians, Christ is seen as unique, transcending all the powers in heaven (who are not forgotten, but have to *bow the knee* and *confess him as Lord* at the end of the story; so they are still probably part of the background, preached about by the counter-mission). Christ is in fact *in the form of God*, and on *equality with God*. We should probably think again in terms of Gen. 1. Christ was the *Image* of the invisible God, so he was in the form of God; and God said, 'Let us make man . . .', so he spoke to his Image on an equality. It is to be noticed that at the end of the story Christ is given a position (a 'name') higher than he had at the beginning, so once more we are not to think of Christ as *God*; but as God's Image he is on a parity with God.

The story of Christ, as Paul tells it, is at first a series of steps downwards. Christ *did not think equality with God a thing to be grasped, emptied himself, took the form of a slave*. These expressions cover what we have come to call the incarnation. Christ held a position equal to God, but he did not hang on to it. The Greek word for *he emptied himself (ekenosen)* has given rise to a theory of what this involved, the Kenotic theory, whereby, it is thought, Christ left his omnipotence and omniscience behind, and retained only the divine love; but there are problems with this approach, and Paul's own thinking remains quite general. His interest rather is in the fact that Christ, by becoming human, put himself under the Law, and so under the authority of the tyrannical *powers*, who treat men as slaves (Gal. 4.3f.), inflicting sickness, deprivations and miseries on them, as in the Book of Job (cf. Rom. 8.35f.).

With the incarnation, then, Christ no longer has the *form of God* but the *form of a slave*, he has *become in the likeness of men*, and *is found in fashion as a man*; and here he takes a second step down – *he humbled himself, becoming obedient until death, death on a cross*. There are two thoughts here. In another passage, Rom. 5, Paul contrasts the obedience of Christ with the disobedience of Adam, and the same thought underlies the word *obedient* here. In Genesis God made man in his Image, and that man, Adam, disobeyed God in the Garden of Eden. Here is Christ, the Last Adam, as Paul calls him (I Cor. 15.45), and he reverses the damage which Adam did, by his total obedience. Now when Adam ate the fruit of the tree, the penalty was death. 'In the day you eat of it, you shall surely die', God had said; and although in his mercy he actually allowed Adam a long life, in the end he was condemned to die, 'Dust you are, and to dust you shall return' (Gen. 3.19). Jesus' obedience has now reversed this process. He was obedient until death; and not just until death – here is the second thought – but to *death on a cross*, the most appalling and humiliating death of all, the death of slaves. Jesus went as low as a man can go, and he went there willingly.

The succession of steps downwards is then crowned with a triumphant *Therefore*. Because of Christ's self-giving to the uttermost, *God highly exalted him, and gave him the name which is above every name.* The exalting is Jesus' resurrection and enthronement in heaven, and the *name* is the title *Lord – every tongue shall confess that Jesus Christ is Lord*. The word *name* is used for a title, as in Heb. 1.4, 'having become as much superior to angels as the *name* he has obtained is more excellent than theirs'. In Hebrews the name is *Son*, but the context is exactly the same. The opening verses of Hebrews also speak of the cross, the exaltation and the superiority to the angelic powers, with a title, first *Son* and later *Lord* (1.10). In both letters Christ is seen as ending the story enthroned, and accepting the homage of the powers, as Lord of heaven, earth and the underworld. Indeed, as we saw in the last chapter, *that at the name of Jesus every knee should bow and every tongue confess that he is Lord* is virtually a quotation from Isa. 45.23, where the words apply to *God* as the LORD. Jesus has now come very close indeed to divinity.

The most famous step, and the most critical for the future of the church, was taken by St John, who opens his Gospel thus:

> In the beginning was the Word, and the Word was with God, and the Word was God. He was in the beginning with God; all things were made through him, and without him was not anything made that was made . . . And the Word was made flesh and dwelt among us, full of grace and truth; we have beheld his glory, glory as of the only Son of the Father.

I mentioned Philo's account of the archangel of many names, Wisdom, Beginning, Image, Word: we have seen Paul developing some of these ideas of an extension of God, the Beginning and the Image, and John takes up another of them, the *Word*. It so happens that the other three terms are all feminine in Greek; but the word

Logos (*Word*) is masculine, and perhaps for this reason seemed more suitable to John.

John lived forty years after Paul, and he is wanting to have it both ways: he wants to keep to the traditional archangel idea, so he says the Word was *with God*; but he also wants to go beyond it, so he says the Word *was God*. Even here we are on unsteady ground, because Philo could speak of the *Logos* being *theos* (*God*), but he would only have meant that it was divine. Philo was a monotheist. But John was a Pauline Christian with more than Pauline ideas, and at the end of his Gospel Thomas will address Jesus after his resurrection as 'My Lord and my God!' John carries Philo and Paul a step further: it is he who has opened the gate to thinking of Jesus as fully divine.

We can still hear the same controversies as in Colossians humming in the background. There is the table-thumping negative: *All things were made through him, and without him was not anything made that was made*. There are other Christians around who claim that creation took place through other heavenly powers than Christ, or who allow him only part of the credit. No, says John, Christ and Christ alone was the Father's agent in it all. There is probably also an issue over the Glory of God. In Exodus Moses asks to see God's Glory, and God does allow this; he hides Moses in a cleft of rock and causes his Glory to pass by him, proclaiming his Name, 'Yahweh, Yahweh, a God merciful and gracious ... full of grace and truth' (Ex. 33.18–34.6). John is referring to this passage when he writes, *we beheld his glory ... full of grace and truth*, and we probably have the echo of another battle. To the Petrines it was *God's* Glory which possessed Jesus for a while (cf. II Cor. 3); for John, Christians beheld *Christ's* glory, *full of grace and truth*.In his first miracle at Cana Jesus manifested *his* glory (John 2. 11); and even before he was born 'Isaiah saw *his* glory and spoke of him' in his famous vision in Isa. 6 (John 12.41). John totally denied the possession idea. He constantly maintains that Jesus was before Abraham (8.48), before creation (17.5): he is *the Word made flesh*.

So although the Paulines were monotheistic Jews, they had something to work with in the Jewish tradition, the idea of an exalted God who acted through intermediaries of a rather vague status, something between archangels and extensions of divinity. Paul was able to find a lodgment in this complex of ideas for a pre-existent

Christ who was the Beginning of Gen. 1.1 or the Image of Gen. 1.26f.; and John was able to take the idea of the Word from the same Creation chapter, and turn it into a familiar mystery. It is Paul who has done the original thinking, as usual, but John whose version of it is read in half a million churches on Christmas Day.

23

Life after Death

We cannot help dying, but we do not want to be extinct. So all over the world people imagine what it may be like for them to continue life after they die; and that included the Greeks and the Jews who made up the New Testament world. But inevitably the ideas differed, and we have to distinguish the resurrection of the body from the immortality of the soul.

The Greeks thought that we were in two parts, so to speak: the body was an envelope in which the real person, the soul, lived. When Socrates was about to drink the hemlock which would kill him, he tried to prove to his friend Phaedo that *his soul was immortal*; so the hemlock could not affect the real Socrates, and he would live on. Greek philosophers sometimes used a tag, *Soma sema*, The body is a tomb: the soul, the *psyche*, was temporarily imprisoned, but would be released at death. An epitaph survives for a woman slave: 'Zosime, before a slave in body only, Has now found freedom in body also'. Her soul had been free already, and now her body too was at rest.

The Jews saw themselves in the light of the Adam story: God had shaped a doll out of clay, and had breathed into it the breath of life, so man had become a living being (*nephesh*). So they were a unity: a person was a body breathing, and the breath was not the soul in the separate, Greek sense. Of course, as the psalm says, 'when thou takest away their breath they die'; but the person is the body, and he then goes down to the underworld, which is called Sheol, and is not a place of torture. By the end of the Old Testament period people began to think that this shadowy post-death existence was not good enough, especially for the martyrs who had given their lives under King Antiochus. The Book of Daniel thinks of the dead as 'asleep in the dust', awakening and coming back to life on earth. This would then be the *resurrection of the body*.

Greek and Jewish ideas mingled around the turn of the era, and we find both notions side by side in the New Testament. Matthew is the most Jewish of the evangelists, and he has them both. He says that after the crucifixion 'the tombs were opened, and many *bodies* of the saints who had *fallen asleep were raised*' (27.52): that is perhaps surprising, but it is a straightforward Jewish resurrection-of-the-body doctrine. On the other hand he also says, 'Do not fear those who kill the *body*, but cannot kill the *soul*; but rather fear him [God] who can destroy both *soul and body* in hell' (10.28). Here the disciples are thought of in the Greek way, with souls separate from their bodies. There is a famous rabbinic parable in which the soul and body are compared to a lame man riding on the back of a blind man to steal figs. Josephus was a Pharisee, and his descriptions of Pharisaic belief in life after death sound plainly Greek.

It is not surprising therefore if many modern Christians are in a bit of a muddle. They say each Sunday in the Creed that they believe in 'the resurrection of the body', but they are happier saying Amen to the collect which asks that 'when our bodies lie in the dust, our souls may rest in peace'. When they go to a Prayer Book funeral they hear St Paul explaining at length that the dead are raised as Christ was, and 'come' with a body; but they know that the real situation is better put in the American song (?hymn), 'John Brown's body lies a-mouldering in the grave, But his soul goes marching on'.

For Jews, the resurrection of the dead was naturally expected to mark the end of the age: there might be another age, the kingdom of God, to follow, or even an intermediate age, a millennium, but it would be the end of the world as we know it. This is why the resurrection of Jesus is so crucial. It marks the end of the age, and it is the 'good news' which the church has to proclaim. There is a problem with it, in that the Book of Daniel had led people to expect that *all* the dead would be raised together, and Jesus alone had been raised so far. But he *had* been raised, and he was clearly the first swallow of summer; the general resurrection would follow soon.

All Christians were agreed that Jesus had been raised from death; as Luke puts it, 'he presented himself [to the apostles] alive after his passion by many proofs, appearing to them during forty days' (Acts 1.3). It is important to notice the *appearing*. The early evidence (Paul, up to 62) contains no references to an empty tomb, or to Jesus' eating, or being touched; I return to these stories in the next chapter. It is all *eye*-evidence, Greek *ophthe*: 'he *appeared* to Cephas, then to the twelve. Then he *appeared* to more than five hundred brethren . . . Then he *appeared* to James, then to all the apostles. Last of all, as to one untimely born, he *appeared* also to me' (I Cor. 15.5–8). Everyone could agree that he had appeared, that they had seen him. What exactly this implied about souls and risen bodies did not need to be defined, and could be left open.

Paul taught consistently the traditional Jewish line. Jesus had risen *physically*, his *body* had been raised; and the same future awaited the ordinary Christian who died. There had been a muddle at Thessalonica. The mission had lasted only a few weeks, and some of the converts had gained the impression that when they were baptized they were inheritors of eternal life, and that this meant they would not die. When one of them did die, the church was understandably shaken, and Paul wrote:

> For since we believe that Jesus died and rose again, even so, through Jesus, God will bring with him those who have fallen asleep . . . For the Lord himself will descend . . . and the dead in Christ will rise first; then we who are alive, who are left, shall be caught up together with them in the clouds, to meet the Lord in the air; and so we shall always be with the Lord (I Thess. 4.14–17).

Jesus died and rose again *bodily*. So the dead Christian, and any who might subsequently die, *have* similarly *fallen asleep*; and Paul is expecting the Lord's coming to be pretty soon, in his own lifetime. When that happens, they will *rise* from their graves, just as in the Book of Daniel. Daniel does not mention what is to happen to the faithful Jews who are still alive at the resurrection, so Paul has to fill in the gap. Daniel 7.13 spoke of one like a son of man coming *with the clouds* to God, so he has warrant for thinking that the Lord will come on clouds. If he is taking dead and resurrected Christians with him to heaven, no doubt he will take us living Christians too. The alarmed and despondent Thessalonians can take heart: their dead brethren will lose nothing.

Five years later Paul was surprised to hear that a different resurrection doctrine was being taught in his church at Corinth. 'How can some of you say that there is no resurrection of the dead?', he asks (I Cor. 15.12). At first we might think that they did not believe in the resurrection *at all*; but this is not so. Jesus' resurrection was the foundation of *every* Christian's faith (as Paul says). The new doctrine becomes clearer in v. 35, 'But someone will ask, How are the dead raised? With what kind of body do they come?' What is being challenged is the *bodily* resurrection theory; it is being objected (not entirely unreasonably) that the old body we had will be nothing but dust and bone in a couple of years, and will not be much on Resurrection Day. Furthermore, we hear that some Corinthians were being *baptized* a second time *on behalf of the dead* (v. 29): so clearly they do believe that the dead live on, and that their relatives can be included in the body of Christ, and so ultimate salvation, if a baptism is performed for them by proxy. So a better translation of v. 12 would be, 'How can some of you say that there is no resurrection of *dead bodies*?': the Greek *nekros* does really mean a corpse.

Who were these people pushing a non-physical idea of resurrection? They are the same people Paul has been arguing with since the beginning of the letter. In ch. 2 they boasted that they were *spiritual*, and here again Paul is insisting that the physical comes before the spiritual: we are still in the physical phase, the spiritual is yet to come (vv. 44–47). In ch. 4 they were saying that the kingdom of God had arrived *already*; and here Paul says stoutly, 'I tell you this, brethren: flesh and blood cannot inherit the kingdom of God' (15.50). In chs 1–2 Paul was attacking the 'taught words of human wisdom', the Jewish traditional interpretations of the Law which were known as *torah*, guidance, in Hebrew, or *sophia*, wisdom, in Greek: here he ends the discussion, 'The sting of death is sin, and the power of sin is *the law*' (15.56). The non-physical resurrection doctrine is an integral part of the teaching of 'those of Cephas' (1.12). They thought the kingdom had come already, that they were already spiritual, even perfect, that in baptism they had been raised from eternal death to eternal life. When they died, their body would lie a-mouldering in the grave, but their soul would go marching on.

But did Peter himself believe this, and James and the others? We do not know. Paul certainly thought he subscribed to the full physical resurrection, because he starts the chapter by speaking as if they all thought the same about it. But in fact 'Jesus appeared to me' can mean one thing to one person and another to another. J. B. Phillips went on record as having seen C. S. Lewis one afternoon after the latter's death: he was the other side of the room, and gave Phillips a signal of encouragement. Phillips *saw* Lewis; but he does not stress that he was there physically, reconstituted flesh and all, and I do not suppose for a moment that that was what he thought. So perhaps Peter just thought that he had seen Jesus 'alive after his passion', without too much theorizing; and perhaps it was him, and perhaps his followers, who laid stress on the spiritual raising. After all, that is the more plausible account; and David Jenkins, the retiring Bishop of Durham, who has read St Paul carefully, is happy to maintain the Petrine position, or something very close to it. Even a modern sophisticate can move from the physical to the spiritual view.

In I Cor. 15 Paul tried to answer the spiritual-resurrection view with four arguments. (1) First he says that Jesus was raised physically, so we will be raised physically too; he gives a list of all the appearances to the apostles to show that this was the united experience of the church. But, as we have just seen, 'he appeared to Cephas' might have been understood 'spiritually' by Peter himself, and certainly was by his disciples at Corinth. (2) The Petrines thought that with Jesus' resurrection had come their own spiritual resurrection. They had been raised with Christ: how would Paul explain that on his theory only Jesus has risen? Paul replies (15.20–28) that Jesus was like the firstfruits, the green wheatsheaf which was cut after Passover (at Easter time) and dedicated in the Temple, so sanctifying the whole crop (the church) which would be raised at (the final) Pentecost. (3) The Petrines derided Paul's physical theory ('With what kind of body do [the dead] come?'), so Paul answers the objection with the idea of a transformed body – the seed dies (so Paul believed), and up comes a transformed seed, a corn shoot. So shall we be transformed into new, glorious bodies (15.35–44). (4) Paul argues from Genesis that Adam was made of clay ('dust') and was perishable, and we are now still perishable too. It is not until the Lord comes that we shall be transformed and made imperishable (15.45–57).

It is not difficult to understand and sympathize with the Petrines, here as in so many other points. With their conversion, dramatized and made effective by baptism, they felt their lives to be transformed. They were seized by the Spirit, they spoke in tongues, they received visions, at their prayers healings took place; they took part in a charismatic fellowship marked with the dedicated sharing of possessions and a lively spirit of joy and expectancy. All this was traced to the resurrection of Jesus; they were risen with him, and the Spirit which had possessed him now possessed them. The new, final age had begun. We find echoes of this belief in other passages of the New Testament. In II Thess. 2.2 Paul begs the church not to be shaken in mind by the claim that 'the day of the Lord has come'. The Jerusalem mission believed that the day of the Lord had come on Easter Day: with Jesus' resurrection the kingdom of God was already present. Half a century later the Pastor complains of Hymenaeus and Philetus, leading Petrines in Ephesus in his day, 'who have swerved from the truth by holding that the resurrection is past already' (II Tim. 2.18). They thought that 'the resurrection' had taken place when Jesus had been spiritually raised; and all true spiritual Christians now shared in this resurrected, transformed life. The word *already* is a constant sign of the Petrine teaching.

Paul is careful to avoid any suggestion that Christians are in any sense already risen. 'Do you not know', he says, 'that all of us who have been baptized into Christ Jesus were baptized into his death? We were buried therefore with him by baptism into death, so that as Christ was raised from the dead by the glory of the Father, we too might walk in newness of life.' (Rom. 6.3f.). We *were baptized into his death*, we *were buried with him*: we might have expected *so that we might be raised with him*, but honest Paul wants moral fruits from his churches – what he puts is, *so that we might walk in newness of life*. He goes on, 'For if we have been united with him in a death like his, we shall certainly be united with him in a resurrection like his' (6.5): we *have been* united with him in a baptismal death, we *shall be* united with him in a resurrection at his Coming. 'But if we have died with Christ, we believe that we shall also live with him' (6.8): our death with him is at our baptism in the past, our living with him in resurrection is still in the future.

Only once does Paul speak of being raised with Christ in the past, and that is at Col. 3.1. He has been debating with the Petrines rather fiercely in ch. 2, attacking their law doctrine, their insistence on sabbath and food and purity rules, their visions and other matters. He continues, 'If then you have been raised with Christ, seek the things that are above . . .': he means *If*, as you pretentiously claim, you are risen with Christ *already*, why don't you live up to your claims and live a decent moral life? (3.5–11) For as soon as a whole group of people get the idea that they are perfect, and above bodily things, it is usually found that somebody in the group begins to feel that ordinary moral standards do not count; that is what happened at Corinth where one of the Petrines slept with (?' married') his (?dead) father's wife (I Cor. 5.1), and people started saying 'Anything goes' ('All things are lawful', 6.13, 10.23), and quarrelling (3.3) and getting drunk (11.21). So here Paul warns the Colossian church, 'Put to death therefore what is earthly in you: fornication, impurity . . . anger, wrath, malice . . .' (Col. 3.5,8). It is ironic that this is much the best known Pauline text on being risen with Christ, for the church has, in all innocence, selected it as the Epistle for Easter Day. So Christians have come to think that Paul taught that they *were already* raised with Christ in baptism; which was the doctrine of his opponents, and exactly the opposite of what he himself believed. Alas for the vanity of all human endeavour! We strive and strain, and would die for our convictions; and when we have won the battle, those who follow us totally misunderstand what we have maintained, and in reading and sermon inculcate in our name the teaching of our opponents!

24

Jesus' Resurrection

The New Testament gives two different forms of evidence for the belief that Jesus rose from the dead. There is *visual* evidence, reports that various people saw him alive after his passion; and there is more concrete, *physical* evidence, reports of people touching him, or of his eating and drinking with them, or of an empty tomb from which his body had disappeared.

It is important to realize the difference in date of these two kinds of evidence. The bulk of the visual evidence, the reports of *appearances*, are so early that it would be absurd to question them (though it is not, of course, absurd to question the interpretations of them). Paul says:

> For I delivered to you as of first importance what I also received, that Christ died for our sins according to the scriptures, that he was buried, that he was raised on the third day in accordance with the scriptures, and that he appeared to Cephas, then to the twelve. Then he appeared to more than five hundred brethren at one time, most of whom are still alive, though some have fallen asleep. Then he appeared to James, then to all the apostles. Last of all, as to one untimely born, he appeared also to me (I Cor. 15.3–8).

These traditions of the six central appearances of Jesus were the core of the Christian good news, the gospel. Paul *delivered* it to the Corinthians when he brought his mission there in 50; and he knew about the other five appearances because he *also received* these traditions himself when he was converted, in about 34. This was only a couple of years after Jesus was crucified, and it is unbelievable that such stories had been made up. They were the tradition in which every Christian was instructed, which he *received*; and they were the basis of the faith which overturned the world. Paul wants to persuade the Corinthians that the leading Petrines agreed with him about Jesus' *bodily* resurrection, so he cites only appearances to Peter, James, the apostles and a mass meeting; he probably knew about Mary Magdalene too, but she is mentioned only in the Gospels.

The *more physical* stories are later: Paul never mentions the empty tomb (though it would have helped his argument to have done so), or the touching, eating and drinking stories. The empty tomb is first mentioned by Mark, about 69. Jesus eats a fish in Luke, about 90, and asks his disciples to handle him (Luke 24.39–41). This touching element receives greater stress with the story of Thomas, which is first found in John about 100 (John 20.24–29). People often think that because these incidents come earlier in the story-sequence than the appearances to the 500, etc., they are more dependable: but no story is more dependable than its first teller, and we have to be careful with stories which first occur forty, sixty or seventy years after the event. Perhaps there has been a development of the tradition, and perhaps there has been a motive for developing it.

When people pass through a crisis, they are liable to see things quite differently from the way they did before, and such changes are commonly accompanied by visual and aural experiences. Many people who are bereaved see their dead partner once or twice in the months after the parting. Religious conversions have often been associated with visions of saints, experiences of bright light, or (as with Augustine) the hearing of voices. Here is an account of such an experience by Susan Atkins, who took part in a dreadful series of murders with Charles Manson in the 1970s:

> The thoughts tumbled over and over in my mind. Can society forgive one for such acts against humanity? Can it take this guilt off my shoulders? Can serving the rest of my life in prison undo what's been done? Can anything be done?
> I looked at my future, my alternatives. Stay in prison. Escape. Commit suicide. As I looked, the wall in my mind was blank. But somehow I knew there was another alternative. I could choose the road many people had been pressing on me. I could follow Jesus.

As plainly as daylight came the words, 'You have to decide. Behold, I stand at the door and knock'. Did I hear someone say that? I assume I spoke in my thoughts, but I'm not certain. 'What door?' 'You know what door and where it is, Susan. Just turn around and open it, and I will come in.' Suddenly, as though on a movie screen, there in my thoughts was a door. It had a handle. I took hold of it and pulled. It opened. The whitest, most brilliant light I had ever seen poured over me. In the center of the flood of brightness was an even brighter light. Vaguely, there was the form of a man. I knew it was Jesus. He spoke to me – literally, plainly, matter-of-factly spoke to me in my 9-by–11 prison cell. 'Susan, I am really coming into your heart to stay.' I was distinctly aware that I inhaled deeply, and then, just as fully, exhaled. There was no more guilt! It was gone. Completely gone! The bitterness, too, instantly gone! How could this be? For the first time in my memory I felt clean, fully clean, inside and out. In 26 years I had never been so happy.[1]

I am not concerned here with the question whether such experiences are experiences *of God*, of the Transcendent; I am merely noting that it is not uncommon for spiritual crises to find their resolution through visions and voices, and that the vision seen, or the voice heard, is normally that of the central figure in the crisis, whether a dead partner, or a saint (often as pictured in a missal), or the leading figure of the particular religious tradition. Perhaps Susan Atkins had a genuine experience of God in a moment of repentance and forgiveness; but she saw Jesus because he was 'the road many people had been pressing on' her. That was how she knew that 'the form of a man' was Jesus. When Ezekiel, rather similarly, saw 'the likeness as it were of a human form' (1.26), he knew that it was Yahweh (1.28).

Today we have psychologists, who collect such experiences and study them, so that we know that they are not rare; to Peter and the first Christians such an event was amazing, and unique. Peter especially had passed through a crisis in Holy Week. He had been the leader among the disciples. He had given up a wife and a living

---

[1]Cited from M. J. Meadow and R. J. Kahoe, *Psychology of Religion*, New York 1984, 90.

to follow Jesus, and had nailed his colours to the mast. He had then suffered a series of humiliations. He had boasted of his faithfulness, and Jesus had prophesied his denials. He had slept in Gethsemane, and had been rebuked. He had forsaken Jesus and fled. He had three times denied his master to save his skin. Finally Jesus, on whom he had pinned such high hopes, died a pathetic death in public. Small wonder if he were in crisis, in need of resolving the same despair and self-horror which we can sense in Susan Atkins' account. It is easy to think that in modern terms what Peter experienced was a *conversion-vision*. On Good Friday Peter could only see himself as a total spiritual failure; and Jesus too – all the hopes of the last years and the talk of the kingdom of God, it had all been an empty dream. The Easter vision cleared all that away. Jesus was alive; the things he had said were true; Peter was a forgiven sinner; the movement had a great future.

We can only interpret the things that happen to us through the categories of thought which our society and upbringing provide to us. Peter had not heard of conversion-visions. He had read the Book of Daniel, and he knew that at the end of history God would raise the dead. If he had seen Jesus, then Jesus was alive, and that meant that the resurrection of the dead had begun. As others of the disciples began to see the Lord also, his conviction became a certainty. The Lord was risen indeed: the new age had begun.

Unfortunately the spreading of an experience does not mean its confirmation at all. When half a dozen people have reported seeing flying saucers, it is found that thousands of others have seen them too. Multitudes of faithful Irishmen will testify to having seen the head move on the statue of the Virgin Mary at Knock. Many Americans in South Dakota claimed to have seen Sasquatch, or Bigfoot, an eight-feet tall, hairy, evil-smelling monster, in 1977. Such stories quickly gain credence, and sightings multiply, in small communities with limited education and under threat – like the early church – especially when there is a psychological pay-off. So it does not add anything important to Peter's experience to hear that five hundred Christians later saw the risen Lord. Under other circumstances they might have seen UFOs, or Bigfoot.

In face of these considerations two defences of traditional belief are usually tried. One is the so-called Beaten Men argument: on

Good Friday the disciples were beaten men, but on Pentecost they proclaimed the resurrection, and were prepared to go to martyrdom for their faith – something must have happened. That is exactly correct. Something had happened, and that was Peter's conversion-vision, followed by similar experiences by other Christians. These visions convinced them that Jesus had risen from death, since that was the explanation offered by Daniel; and naturally they proclaimed this conviction with force and courage.

Alternatively it may be said that psychological explanations do not exclude theological ones: maybe Peter's experience can be explained, or at least paralleled, from other crisis experiences, but that does not prevent it also being a real experience of the risen Jesus. Such arguments are suspect, for we do not need two competing explanations for events, and in such cases generally this-worldly explanations have been shown to be preferable. Suppose a man fell down foaming at the mouth. One person might say, 'He has a demon', and another, 'It is an epileptic fit'. With drugs the patient is restored to normality, so the epilepsy explanation seems right; but it might be said, 'Yes: the epilepsy was caused by a demon'. If we can do without supernatural second explanations, we should do so.

At first Christians were content to be united over the wonder of the resurrection: it was enough that leading Christians had *seen* Jesus. But by the 50s, as we saw in the last chapter, there were divisions over whether Jesus had risen *physically* (as Paul thought), or *spiritually*, as the Jerusalem mission held. We find this split continuing into the second century. Ignatius, a Pauline, has visited various churches in Asia (W. Turkey), and writes to the church at Smyrna to counter Jewish-Christian possessionist views:

> For I know and believe that (Jesus Christ) was in the flesh even after the resurrection; and when he came to Peter and his company, he said to them, *Lay hold and handle me, and see that I am not a demon without body.* And straightaway they touched him, and they believed, being joined unto his flesh and his blood . . . And after his resurrection, he ate and drank with them as one in the flesh, though spiritually he was united with the Father (*Smyrn.* 3).

The Jerusalem Christians thought that Christ had left the human Jesus on the cross, and that Christ, as an angelic power, was spiritual; Jesus had risen from the dead and had gone to heaven, the realm of spiritual beings – so his resurrection was non-physical. Ignatius followed Paul in believing that Jesus-Christ was a single being: if he was risen, then his *body* was risen, and that meant that the resurrection experiences were of Jesus' body as well as his soul. Ignatius makes use of Luke's Gospel to prove this. The touching and eating themes come in Luke 24; and Luke 24.39 actually says, *Handle me and see, for a spirit does not have flesh and bones, as you see me having.* Ignatius has altered the last part of the quotation, because *a demon without body* sounds worse than *a spirit not having flesh and bones.*

Ignatius was writing about 115, and he draws on Luke, who wrote about 90. It seems suspiciously convenient that these stories, so recently produced, should just answer to Ignatius' needs. Luke knew that Jesus had appeared 'first to Cephas, then to the Twelve', so he has elaborated the tradition a little to make it clear that the Pauline teaching was right. The disciples are gathered in the evening, and know about the appearance to Peter (Luke 24.34); at first they are terrified and 'thought they were seeing a spirit' (24.37). You see, Peter and the others got hold of the wrong end of the stick from the start; but actually Jesus showed them that he was there in body, *having flesh and bones, as you see me having.* It is the preacher's duty to explain the tradition in such a way that his congregation understand its true meaning. The broiled fish, and the touching, and later (in John) the Thomas story, all fix in the minds of the faithful the essential Pauline doctrine: Jesus rose *physically.*

And what about Mark twenty years earlier? We know the issue was being fought out before Mark, because we have it argued in I Corinthians, about 55. Mark did not think to include any Appearance stories, but he took up from Paul the detail, *that he was buried.* We must suppose that Mark had some tradition about Joseph of Arimathaea, and about Mary Magdalene wishing to anoint the Lord's dead body. But the story carries the same point which Luke was making in an earlier phase. The angel says to the women, 'Do not be amazed; you seek Jesus of Nazareth who was crucified. He has risen, he is not here; see the place where they laid him.' You see, Jesus' body had disappeared; he was risen *physically*; the place where he had been laid was empty.

But was this Mark's piece of embroidery too, or was this an old tradition going back to the women themselves? The answer seems to lie in the surprising end to Mark's Gospel. The resurrection is clearly the climax of the book, and three times Jesus has foretold it, so the reader is expecting it. He is also expecting a triumphant note for the Gospel to end on. The women have been told to go and tell Peter and the others to go to Galilee where they will see Jesus (16.7); so all that is necessary is for them to do as they are told, and the story will be complete. The puzzle is that this does not happen. Mark ends, 'And they went out and fled from the tomb; for trembling and astonishment had come upon them; and they said nothing to anyone, for they were afraid' (16.8).

If the women said nothing to anyone, the question arises, How did the disciples know to go back to Galilee? The story contains a contradiction, which needs explaining. Now suppose that Mark has applied his creative imagination, telling this story in his church in the 60s for the first time. Will there not be veteran Christians sitting in the congregation who will be thinking, I have been a Christian twenty years and it is the first time I have heard this? Perhaps some of them are Petrine Christians who do not believe that Jesus rose physically at all; are they not likely to object, Where does this story come from? So Mark is ready with his answer. He has been lucky enough to hear about all this in a roundabout way quite recently, but it has never been public before. You see, brethren, the women panicked when they had seen the angel – you know what women are like; *for trembling and astonishment had come upon them; and they said nothing to anyone, for they were afraid.*

So we have reason to think that the more concrete elements in the tradition, the eating, drinking, touching and empty tomb themes, are a later development: they arise from the controversy with the Petrine, spiritual-resurrection view, and are composed by Pauline evangelists, Mark, Luke and John, to support the physical-resurrection doctrine. The visual evidence is from much earlier, and goes back to the events immediately following the crucifixion. But they should be understood today as internal events. Jesus did not really rise from the dead, either physically or spiritually. Rather his followers had conversion-visions which they interpreted in line with the biblical categories of their time.

25

The Noise of Battle

The curtain rises on our Tale of Two Missions with Paul's account in Gal. 2 (ch. 1 above). At this point, in 48, the Pauline mission consisted of some six or seven churches: the established church at Antioch in North Syria, and (on Luke's authority, Acts 13f.) a little string of newly founded churches in Cyprus, Pisidia and Galatia (South and Central Turkey). The Galatian churches, to whom Paul was writing, were at towns called Iconium, Derbe and Lystra. At this time the Pauline mission probably numbered about three hundred members.

It is not so easy to picture the growth of the Jerusalem mission. There was plainly a large Jewish Christian church in Jerusalem, and we hear of churches in Lydda and Joppa, towns in Judaea, in Galilee, and further afield in Caesarea, Damascus and Alexandria. Luke gives us some optimistic figures – 3,000 on the day of Pentecost alone, later 5,000, 'many tens of thousands' (Acts 21.20). Perhaps: but not, I think, *many* tens of thousands. It suffices to say that the church got off to a strong start in its home area.

Luke's account in Acts is the only report we have of the church's early history, and it takes us only as far as Paul's arrival in Rome, about 60. After that we have a long gap: Eusebius, Bishop of Caesarea in the fourth century, and a toady of the Emperor Constantine, wrote a *History of the Church* which includes many letters and excerpts of earlier writings, and we have to do our best to piece things together, especially in the early period, where his information is naturally thinnest. He relates a revealing story of a controversy which took place about 190. The churches were divided over the details of the fasting and celebration of what we would call Holy Week, and an attempt was made to settle the matter by the leading bishops:

Eusebius had read the letters which survived to his day from these various leaders (*Ecclesiastical History* 5.23). Now a part of the fascination of this account is that it shows us the scope of the church at this date.

On the one side (fast till Saturday, feast on Easter Day) were the main body of churches: the bishops of Caesarea and Jerusalem in Palestine, Victor, Bishop of Rome (who tried to throw his weight about), the bishops of Pontus (North Turkey), Gaul (including Irenaeus, Bishop of Lyons, who saw a compromise through), Osroene (South-east Turkey), Corinth and 'great numbers of others'. On the other side (fast till 13th Nisan, feast on 14th, when the Passover lamb was sacrificed, on whichever day of the week it fell), were the bishops of 'the whole of Asia' (probably the rest of Turkey), led by Polycrates, Bishop of Ephesus. The interest lies partly in the areas which are *not* mentioned. The 'catholics' are represented by the churches of France, Italy (Rome), Greece (Corinth), outlying parts of Turkey (Pontus and Osroene), and the two Palestinian dioceses; the Asians probably cover the rest of Turkey.

But where are the great dioceses of Syria and Egypt – Antioch, Damascus, Alexandria, and points east? They are missing; and if they had written among 'the great numbers of others', we may be sure that Eusebius would have cited them. The likely conclusion is that *they were not part of Christendom*, as Victor and Polycrates understood it: they were heretical, *Ebionites*, as Irenaeus would have described them. To us, attempting a more neutral stance, the churches involved were the churches of the old Pauline mission, now the majority church recognizing only Pauline orthodoxy. The churches of Palestine, Syria and Egypt were the descendants of the Jerusalem mission, with a now outmoded Petrine theology. The only dioceses Eusebius mentions in this vast area are in the Greek (non-Jewish) cities of Caesarea and Jerusalem (Jerusalem was forbidden to Jews after the War in 70). In the third century the Paulines would win over most of the Christians of these provinces, reducing the rump to the status of moribund deviants.

So the Paulines triumphed in the end; and that is why Christians generally do not keep the kosher rules, or sabbath today; or share their money, or cease working, or give up sex for ascetic reasons; or think that Jesus was possessed by a Spirit from his baptism till his passion. Their creed is the Pauline creed and their New Testament is the Pauline Epistles and the three Pauline Gospels, Mark, Luke and John, and the Pauline Acts; supplemented by 'bridge' writings, Matthew, James and the Apocalypse. It would be interesting to know the detail of how the Paulines won.

The visit of Peter to Antioch (Gal. 2.11–14, ch. 1 above) was a disaster for Paul. 'Even Barnabas was carried away by their hypocrisy', and now that the chips were down, all the Jewish members sided with Peter. If Paul had defied Peter, the Jerusalem church would have disowned him; they would have split his Cypriot and Galatian churches as they had his Antiochene mother-church, taking the Jewish members with them, and leaving the Gentiles to rot. He swallowed the bitter alternative, with a bad grace ('I withstood Cephas to the face'). His Gentile converts must have kosher meat for their Saturday supper, and keep quiet about working on sabbath. They were lucky not to be forced into circumcision. A chastened Barnabas went back to Cyprus to impose the new discipline, and Paul, setting out on a second mission, had to submit to the indignity of being supervised by a Jerusalem Christian, Silas. When they came to Paul's mission church at Derbe, he was forced to have his half-Gentile convert Timothy circumcised (Acts 16.1–3).

Luke says that the Holy Ghost forbade Paul to speak the word in Asia, or Bithynia (North-west Turkey), but called him in a vision over to Macedonia (North Greece); the Holy Spirit had the idea that the further any new Pauline churches were from Jerusalem, the better chance they would stand of not being interfered with by zealous Petrines. As it was, the uneasy partnership of Paul and Silas soon broke up. Paul went down to Corinth while Silas remained in Macedonia, and when Silas joined him, it was not for long; he disappears from the account in Acts, and in Paul's letters. It is clear, however, that he had wrought a good deal of mischief in the Macedonian churches. The Thessalonian mission, for example, had lasted only a few weeks, but had included Silas' encouragement to the converts to give up work, and to believe that the day of the Lord had already come; Paul had had to speak about these matters at the time: 'as we charged you' (I Thess. 4.11), 'when I was still with you' (II Thess. 2.5; 3.10), and to write two letters – with Silas' reluctant agreement – to put things straight. It is likely that Silas went back to

Jerusalem in 51 and had further Petrine evangelists sent to Corinth; who caused all the trouble underlying our two Corinthian letters.

Paul settled in Ephesus, in Asia, from 52 to 55, and it was in these years that his mission was under the strongest pressure, and that the future of the Christian religion was settled. The Ephesian mission was a success. Paul wrote, 'A wide door for effective work has opened to me, and there are many adversaries' (I Cor. 16.9); and he stayed in the place three years (Acts 20.31), longer than any other of his missions. But the adversaries – the Petrines – got the upper hand in the end, and Paul left the city in a virtual breakdown (II Cor. 1.8, 'we were so utterly, unbearably crushed that we despaired of life itself'). The Pastor wrote later, in Paul's name, drawing on well-known memories, 'all who are in Asia turned away from me' (II Tim. 1.15). Luke, keen to keep any division in the church quiet, describes Paul's journey to Jerusalem in 57: 'when he met us at Assos [north of Ephesus], we took him on board . . . we came to Miletus [south of Ephesus]. For Paul had decided to sail past Ephesus, so that he might not have to spend time in Asia' (Acts 20.13–16). Paul began the journey as a passenger, but he appears to have bought the boat during the journey! And he is in a great hurry, so he sails past Ephesus; but in the next verses he has time to send from Miletus to Ephesus to summon his Ephesian elders to come to him for a farewell sermon, which must have taken an extra week! It is obvious that Paul was *persona non grata* at his flagship church at Ephesus, and dared not show his face there.

While Paul was at Ephesus, the Petrines stepped up the attack on his other churches. They arrived in Galatia with the slogan, 'Circumcision alone is the passport to heaven', and appealed, as we have seen (ch. 4), to the Bible as God's word. Hitherto the Jerusalem approach had been to insist on practical matters, the food and other purity laws, sabbath and the Jewish festivals: but now they are going, metaphorically, for the jugular. Here for the first time the Pauline line held. Loyalty to their missioner combined with distaste for the knife; the elders of the little group of churches conferred, and wrote to their apostle; and when they received his angry, opaque but firm reply (our Galatians), they said No to the Petrines.

In the meantime other Jerusalem delegates arrived in Corinth, and created major dissension in the church there. They contrasted

Paul's frail claims to apostleship with those of Peter, their authority; they insisted on Jewish ways ('taught words of human wisdom'), on sexual asceticism, and on the kingdom of God, and a spiritual resurrection, having already arrived. Paul wrote a kindly, fatherly letter (I Corinthians), criticizing these ideas, and also drawing attention to various excesses which disgraced the church. In 54 he followed this up with a disastrous visit to the church: one of the leading Petrines defied and insulted Paul, and the church did not support the apostle. He wrote a depressed letter (II Cor. 2.9; 7.8), which in fact turned the tide; and when he had been driven out of Ephesus, he was comforted to learn from his lieutenant Titus that the Corinthians were standing by him. These two unnamed groups of elders, at Corinth and in Galatia in Central Turkey, changed the course of history. Their support of Paul enabled his mission to survive its moment of acute weakness, and to become a world religion; Petrine Christianity could never have been more than a short-lived sect of Judaism.

Paul spent the winter of 56/57 in Corinth, and wrote Romans, a long, contradictory, but enormously impressive statement of his 'gospel'; he did not want the same trouble in the capital of the Roman world, where a church had been founded and was flourishing; he intended to stop over there before evangelizing Spain. But this was not to be. In 57 he went to Jerusalem with a large collection which he had been taking up from the Gentile churches for the impoverished Metropolitan church. But feeling had moved a long way since he had engaged to do this in 48. The resistance in Galatia and Corinth, with Paul's connivance, showed that he was a reprobate and a heretic. His money was refused, and it was with Jewish Christian collusion that he was attacked in the Temple, nearly lynched, imprisoned and finally sent to Rome to his martyrdom.

Before Paul died he received some happy news. One of his converts, Epaphras, had carried the Pauline message up country in Asia, and had started new churches in the valley of the Lycus river, in Colosse, Laodicea and Hierapolis. Paul was in chains, but he could write still, and his last letters, to the churches at Colosse and Laodicea (our Ephesians), and to Philemon, a leading Christian at Colosse, show both that the Pauline mission is spreading, and that the Petrines are there as well. The battle was hard fought, all along the line.

As Tertullian was to say 150 years later, the blood of the martyrs is the seed of the church (*sanguis martyrum semen Ecclesiae*); and once Paul was put to death, there was a strong revulsion of feeling in his favour. He had also laid a good foundation of ordaining elders in each church, so that even when the Petrines had the following of a majority of church members, the committee was normally Pauline. So the Macedonian, Corinthian and Galatian churches formed a block of communities loyal to Paul; and the Roman churches roughly followed, though they ended by having it both ways. It was in Asia, and especially around Ephesus, that the battle was hardest fought. Of our New Testament documents, Galatians, Ephesians, Colossians, Philemon, the Pastorals, I Peter, the Gospel of John, the three letters of John and the Apocalypse are all written by Paulines or semi-Paulines against Petrines in Asia Minor. So are the letters of Ignatius (115). This is some explanation of the line-up of bishops in 190: Polycrates of Ephesus is the spokesman for Pauline churches in Asia, but they have inherited Jerusalem liturgical practices which are suspect to the rest of Pauline christendom.

The Jerusalem mission reached the height of its power in the 50s. Its own leader, James, was martyred, like Paul, in 62, and it received a heavy blow in the second half of the decade. From 66 to 70 the Jewish people rebelled against Rome, and in 70 Jerusalem was taken with great loss of life. This included many Christians, whose 'dead bodies lay in the streets of the great city where their Lord was crucified' (Rev. 11.8). The leadership which survived had to move, for Jerusalem became a city forbidden to Jews; and the financial troubles are likely to have been exacerbated. But the fight went on, and the Pastorals and the writings of John both display a bitterness of feeling which we never had in Paul, and which shows the two wings of the church losing charity to one another, and moving towards excommunication and heresy-hunting.

We can trace the progress of the battle from the comments on the various Asian churches, first in Paul in the 50s, then in the Apocalypse in the 80s, and then in Ignatius, with hints from elsewhere. Paul was driven out of Ephesus, but there are still Pauline elders there whom he calls to Miletus in Acts 20. Revelation gives the church high marks: 'I know your works, your toil and your patient endurance, and how you cannot bear evil men but have tested those [Petrines] who call themselves apostles but are not . . .' (Rev. 2.2). But some of the sparkle has gone out of church life: 'I have this against you, that you have abandoned the love you had at first' (2.4). The writings of John, which Irenaeus says came from Ephesus, show a divided church: indeed some members have left the church – 'they went out from us, but they were not of us' (I John 2.19). Nevertheless, the Pauline mission was gaining the upper hand, and it could produce one of the church's great theologians in St John, author of Gospel and Epistles (but not the Apostle John, nor the Beloved Disciple). Ignatius treats it as the capital of the church in Asia, writing (greasily and untruthfully) that the sainted Paul mentions it in every letter; and that is how we find things when Polycrates wrote his letter to Victor in 190.

We may contrast the situation in up-country Laodicea. Epaphras founded the church about 60, and Paul wrote to it soon afterwards. The letter is preserved as our Ephesians, but the name is missing in the oldest manuscripts, and about 150 a deviant Christian called Marcion referred to it as written to Laodicea. It shows clearly that Paul does not know the church members, which would not be the case at Ephesus, where he ran the church for three years. So it is likely that the church went over to the Petrines, and did not value Paul's letter; and a Pauline Christian took it to Ephesus. The Laodicean church is the worst of the seven churches in Asia addressed in the Apocalypse: 'I know your works: you are neither cold nor hot . . . because you are lukewarm, and neither cold nor hot, I will spew you out of my mouth' (Rev. 3.15f.). When Ignatius passed through Asia on his way to the lions at Rome, the faithful Pauline churches sent delegates to greet and encourage him. The churches included Philadelphia, not far away; but Laodicea was not one of them, and he may actually have passed through the town.

The churches which come best out of the Letters in Rev. 2–3 are Ephesus, Smyrna and Philadelphia; and these, with the smaller churches of Magnesia and Tralles, are the Pauline churches which supported Ignatius – especially Smyrna, with its famous, long-lived bishop, Polycarp, who was martyred forty years later. The Petrines took over some of the valley churches; but the Paulines held the line along the coast and ultimately drove the Jerusalem loyalists out as heretics – Ebionites or Gnostics. I will not say that the meek inherited the earth, for some Paulines were arrogant men; but Paul himself was a humble man, a hero and a saint. Perhaps we could say that historic Christianity owes even more to him than to Jesus.

We should never lose sympathy with the Jerusalem Christians; they lost the great battle, but not for want of devotion or energy. They took the label 'of Cephas', the Petrines, because Peter had been Jesus' leading disciple; but the real leader of the Jerusalem church in the vital period from 40 to 60 was James, Jesus' brother. He must have been a man of great spiritual force. He was not even a disciple in Jesus' lifetime, but he established himself as the church's leader in Jerusalem. He stood out for principle, where Peter was weak-kneed; the Law was God's Law, and must be obeyed, however inconvenient. He was famous for his ascetic life, and he made good relations with the Pharisees in Judaism. He saw the church efficiently organized with envoys ('apostles') to go round and see that standards were maintained. He received the crown of martyrdom. As a 'loser' he has been rather forgotten in church life; but someone who has not been forgotten is his mother Mary. We may think that the praises heaped on her have been somewhat exaggerated, and perhaps she never became Queen of Heaven or Co-Redeemer of mankind. But she is not undeserving of the highest earthly honours: with two such sons, she must have been a formidable woman.

The last we hear of Peter in the Bible is at his Antioch visit in 48: after that he disappears into legend. He probably never went near Rome, for there is no suggestion of his having been there either in Acts or in Paul's letter to the Romans. The Petrines were the losing side, but the Paulines could not do without Peter's name; for they needed to show that they were successors to Jesus' original disciples, of whom he was the best known. So Peter is a sort of stumbling hero, even in the Pauline Gospels of Mark and Luke and John. In the last he is always outshone by the Pauline hero, the Beloved Disciple, though even there he has his place. But Matthew was (christology apart) a Petrine, and it is in Matthew's Gospel that Peter is given the keys of the kingdom. The Roman church wisely adopted Matthew's Gospel as its title deed, and elected Peter posthumously as its first

Pope; for the church of Rome has, from the beginning, been enthusiastic not only for the kingdom, but also for the power and the glory.

Appendix I:

A Table of Dates

The dates given below are all approximate. Those in the left hand column, which refer to the secular Roman world, are the most accurate. Those in the middle column are of events in the Christian communities, and are based partly on column 1 and partly on information inferred from New Testament documents, especially Acts. Where there is a clash between Paul's own account and Acts, Paul has been preferred. The third column, giving dates for the New Testament documents, is inferred from details in the texts, and from the use of one document by another. There is considerable difference between scholars on dating; for another view of the Pauline period the reader may compare Robert Jewett, *Dating Paul's Life* (SCM Press, London and Fortress Press, Philadelphia 1979).

[*G* = Galatians, *A* = Acts, *C* = Corinthians, *Th* = Thessalonians, *R* = Romans]

30 Tiberius Emperor	Jesus crucified
31	
32	
33	
34	Paul converted (*G* 1.15f., *A* 9.1–19)
35	Paul in Arabia (*G* 1.17)
36	Paul in Arabia (*G* 1.17)

37	Gaius (Caligula) Emperor Aretas IV in Damascus	Paul in Damascus (*G* 1.17, *C* 11.32f. *A* 9.20–24)	
38		Paul to Tarsus and Antioch (*G* 1.21, *A* 9.30)	
39			
40			
41	Claudius Emperor, Herod Agrippa I king in Jerusalem		
42			
43		James bar-Zebedee martyred (*A* 12.1f.)	
44	Herod dies (*A* 12.20.23)		
45			
46		Paul & Barnabas in Cyprus (*A* 13.1–12)	
47		Paul & Barnabas in Galatia (*A* 13.13–14.28)	
48		Jerusalem Conference (*G* 2.1–10, *A* 15.1–29) Dispute at Antioch (*G* 2.11–14) Paul and Silas through Galatia (*A* 15.6–16.6)	
49	Claudius expels rioters from Rome	to Philippi, Thess. (I *Th*; *A* 16.7–17.15) Paul at Athens (I *Th* 3.1, *A* 17.16–34)	
50		Paul at Corinth (*A* 18.1–11)	*I Thessalonians*
51	Gallio to Corinth	Paul leaves Corinth (*A* 18.12)	*II Thessalonians*

52		Paul to Ephesus (*A* 19.1–10)	
53		Paul in Ephesus	
54	Nero Emperor	Paul in Ephesus	*I Corinthians*
		Paul visits Corinth (*II C* 7.12)	*Galatians*
55		Paul leaves Ephesus (Troas (II *C* 1; *A* 19.21–40)	
56		Paul in Maced. (II *C* 1f.), Corinth	*II Corinthians* *Romans*
57	Felix procurator	Paul to Jerusalem (*R* 15.22–23, *A* 20–24)	
58		Paul to Caesarea	
59	Festus procurator	Paul to Malta (*A* 25–27)	
60		Paul to Rome (*A* 28)	*Philemon, Colossians*
61		Paul in Rome	*Ephesians*
62		Paul martyred	*Philippians*
		James martyred in Jerusalem	
63			
64	Fire in Rome: Christians blamed by Nero		
65			*Hebrews*
66	Jewish Uprising		
67			
68	Nero killed: year of four Emperors		
69	Vespasian Emperor		*Mark*
70	Fall of Jerusalem	Christians massacred in Jerusalem (*Rev.* 11.7f.)	

71		
72		
73	Pliny's comet	
74		
75		*Matthew*
76		
77		
78		
79	Titus Emperor. Eruption of Vesuvius	
80	Rumours of Nero come to life	
81	Domitian Emperor	*Revelation*
82		
83		
84		
85	Sanhedrin decrees 'Blessing' of heretics	
86		
87		
88		
90		*Luke*
91		
92		
93		
94		*Acts*
95		
96	Nerva Emperor	
97		
98	Trajan Emperor	
99		
100		*John*

Appendix II:

The Standing of This Book

If the reader has come so far, I may hope that s/he has been interested; and if s/he knows anything about the New Testament, s/he will know that what s/he has been reading is not an amalgam of standard opinions. It is what I think. But non-professional readers will want to know how such a picture as I have drawn stands, alongside the views of other scholars; and they have the right to know where to go to follow the matter up if they wish to.

The New Testament was written a long time ago, and we have no access to the communities which produced it other than through its pages. It is inevitable therefore that it should present a mass of problems which are regularly debated in books and in the learned journals. It would be satisfying if we could find a *unitary solution* to these problems, that is, a single theory that would explain them all; and that is what I have tried to propose in this book. But of course there might not be a unitary solution: there might be one problem in Corinth and another in Ephesus and so on. There is no agreed unitary solution at the moment; in general, scholars are content to try to solve one problem at a time. An account of the general state of opinion is available in Werner Kümmel's *An Introduction to the New Testament* (SCM Press, London and Philadelphia, Westminster Press 1965, and later editions).

The theory I have proposed – the Two-Missions hypothesis – is not new in principle: it was in fact suggested in outline by Ferdinand Baur, Professor at Tübingen in Germany, in an article of 156 pages in 1831, and it was broadly accepted during most of the last century. However, Baur made many mistakes, as his successors came to realize, and two major problems for his view were set out by W. Lütgert in 1908. So Baur's theory came to be discredited, and it was temporarily replaced by other unitary hypotheses, which have also in time come to seem implausible.

I found answers to Lütgert's difficulties, and worked out many modifications to Baur's proposal during the 1980s. I read my own suggestions to learned Conferences, and published the papers in professional journals from 1991, especially *New Testament Studies* (*NTS*), the *Journal for the Study of the New Testament* (*JSNT*), the *Scottish Journal of Theology* (*SJT*), and *Novum Testamentum* (*NT*); and in books of essays published in honour of various scholars. The reader will find these journals in most University and other major libraries; or local libraries may order copies on request. These articles give much more detailed arguments than has been possible in this book, and there are many references to opposing opinions, and where they may be read. I give a list of these articles.

On Paul:

'Σοφία in I Corinthians', *NTS* 37 (1991), 516–34 (replying to Lütgert)

'The Visionaries of Laodicea', *JSNT* 43 (1991), 15–39 (on Ephesians)

'Exegesis of Gen. 1–3 in the New Testament', *Journal of Jewish Studies* 43.2 (1992), 226–9
(especially on Col. 1)

'Silas in Thessalonica', *JSNT* 48 (1992), 87–106 (on I and II Thessalonians)

'The Integrity of II Cor. 6.14–7.1', *NT* (1994)
(on II Corinthians)

'Already?', *Essays in Honour of Robert Gundry* (1994) (on two views of the kingdom of God)

'The Phasing of the Future', *Essays in Honour of Lars Hartman* (1995) (on II Thess. 2; Mark 13 and Rev. 8–9)

On Mark:

'Those Outside (Mark 4.10–12)', *NT* 33 (1991), 289–301 (on Jesus' family)

'A Pauline in a Jacobite Church', *The Four Gospels 1992: Essays in*

Honour of Frans Neirynck, BETL 100, ed. F. van Segbroeck, Leuven 1992, II, 859–76 (on 'the Pharisees')
'The Pre-Marcan Gospel', *SJT* (1994) (on the 'Ebionite' Gospel)

On John:

'Nicodemus', *SJT* 44 (1991), 153–68 (on the Jewish Christians)
'John 1.1–2.12 and the Synoptics', *John and the Synoptics*, BETL 101, ed. A. Denaux, Leuven 1992, 201–37, with Appendix: John 2.13–5.54 and the Synoptics (on the Two Missions, applied to John)
'An Old Friend Incognito', *SJT* 45 (1993), 487–513 (on the Beloved Disciple)